ALL ABOUT
SOUPS & STEWS

Joy
of
Cooking

ALL ABOUT
SOUPS & STEWS

IRMA S. ROMBAUER
MARION ROMBAUER BECKER
ETHAN BECKER

PHOTOGRAPHY BY TUCKER & HOSSLER

SCRIBNER
NEW YORK • LONDON • TORONTO • SYDNEY • SINGAPORE

SCRIBNER
1230 Avenue of the Americas
New York, NY 10020

WELDON OWEN INC.
Chief Executive Officer: John Owen
President: Terry Newell
Chief Operating Officer: Larry Partington
Vice President, International Sales: Stuart Laurence
Publisher: Roger Shaw
Creative Director: Gaye Allen
Associate Publisher: Val Cipollone
Art Director: Jamie Leighton
Production Director: Stephanie Sherman
Consulting Editors: Judith Dunham, Norman Kolpas
Assistant Editor: Anna Mantzaris
Studio Manager: Brynn Breuner
Pre-press Coordinator: Mario Amador
Production Manager: Chris Hemesath
Food Stylist: Jeff Tucker
Prop Stylist: Sara Slavin
Food Styling Assistants: Rebecca Broder, Angela Kearney
Step-by-Step Photographer: Chris Shorten
Step-by-Step Food Stylist: Kim Brent

Joy of Cooking All About series was designed
and produced by Weldon Owen Inc.,
814 Montgomery Street, San Francisco,
California 94133

Set in Joanna MT and Gill Sans

Separations by Bright Arts Singapore
Printed in Singapore by Tien Wah Press (Pte.) Ltd.

10 9 8 7 6 5 4 3 2 1

Library of Congress Cataloging-in-Publication Data
is available.

ISBN 0-7432-0210-4

Recipe shown on half-title page: *New York Deli Borscht*, 48
Recipe shown on title page: *Fresh Tomato Soup*, 51

CONTENTS

FOREWORD

"Making the pot smile." My Granny Rom and my mother enjoyed quoting the English translation of the French phrase in early editions of the Joy of Cooking *to describe the gentle simmering required for soups and stews. Soups and stews have the power to bring smiles not just to the pot but also to the people who eat them.*

That's why an entire volume of the new All About *series is devoted to soups and stews.* All About Soups & Stews *offers information on key ingredients, along with recipes for a wide variety of stocks, embellishments, and accompanying breads—everything you need whether you're just starting dinner with soup or making a robust stew the centerpiece of your meal.*

You might notice that this collection of kitchen-tested recipes is adapted from the latest edition of the Joy of Cooking. *Just as our family has done for generations, we have worked to make this version of* Joy *a little bit better than the last. As a result, you'll find that some notes, recipes, and techniques have been changed to improve their clarity and usefulness. Since 1931, the* Joy of Cooking *has constantly evolved. And now, the* All About *series has taken* Joy *to a whole new stage, as you will see from the beautiful color photographs of finished dishes and clearly illustrated instructions for preparing and serving them. Granny Rom and Mother would have been delighted.*

I'm sure you'll find All About Soups & Stews *to be both a useful and an enduring companion in your kitchen.*

Enjoy!

Ethan Becker pictured with his grandmother, Irma von Starkloff Rombauer (left), and his mother, Marion Rombauer Becker (right). Irma Rombauer published the first Joy of Cooking at her own expense in 1931. Marion Rombauer Becker became coauthor in 1951. Joy as it has progressed through the decades (from top left to bottom right): the 1931 edition with Marion's depiction of St. Martha of Bethany, said to be the patron saint of cooking, "slaying the dragon of kitchen drudgery"; the 1943 edition; the 1951 edition; the 1962 edition; the 1975 edition; and the 1997 edition.

About Soups & Stews

If any foods seem inherently calming, and even consoling, they are soup and stew. Soups and stews feel good when the weather gets cold. They restore our spirit and our vigor. (The first "restaurants" were eighteenth-century Parisian establishments that served rich soups to restore, or *restaurer*, the hungry citizenry.) In the old days, when a "soup bunch" of vegetables and herbs cost a nickel and bones were free from the local butcher, American home cooks routinely made soups from scratch. Today, the smell of a wonderful soup or a hearty stew simmering on the stove in the kitchen still symbolizes home cooking.

Tools for Making Stocks, Soups, and Stews

The basic tools for making stocks, soups, and stews are a wooden spoon, a ladle, and, of course, a pot. An 8- to 10-quart pot (**1**) is required for making stock (see *About Stocks & Broths*, 13) or large batches of soup or stew. A 4-quart pot is about right for everyday use.

The best type is narrow, tall, and heavy-bottomed, to allow the stock, soup, or stew to simmer gently without too much evaporation and to facilitate skimming.

For making stock, just be sure the pot is large enough to accommodate all of the solids (bones, shells, or vegetables) with room to cover them with 2 inches of water. Dutch ovens (**2**) or wide soup pots also work, as long as you monitor the simmering stock and add more water whenever the level drops below the solids. Using an 8- to 10-quart stockpot will yield 2- to 4-quart batches of stock. Avoid aluminum pots, which may react with the ingredients and affect the flavor. A second large pot is handy for cooling strained stock; plastic containers work, but they insulate, and so the stock will not cool as quickly.

For making brown stocks, it is also essential to have a large roasting pan, preferably with handles. Sieves are another must—ideally two of them, one coarse and one fine. The long-handled conical kind, called a chinois or China cap (**3**), is ideal, but you can improvise a fine-mesh sieve by lining a colander with a double layer of cheesecloth, a dampened layer of paper towels, or a coffee filter. Gravy separators, also called fat separators, are a convenient way to remove excess fat from stock when there is no time to chill the stock and let the fat solidify.

Equipment for Making Soups

Some soups in this book are pureed to make them smooth; others are partially pureed to give them a "creamier" texture. Here are the pros and cons to using commonly available kitchen equipment to adjust the texture of a soup.

Food Processor: This tool is especially good for thick soups. Beware of overloading, as liquids can leak out the bottom or overflow. Depending on the size of your food processor, it may be best to puree soups in two batches. Or you can puree the solid ingredients with just enough

liquid to keep the blade from clogging; return the puree to the pot, and stir or whisk to blend.

Blender (1): A blender works well for pureeing thinner soups. When blending hot soup, do not fill the blender more than one-third full. Wrap a dish towel around the lid and start on a low speed, then gradually increase the speed.

Hand-Held Immersion Blender (2): This tool is exceptionally convenient, because it is portable and easy to clean. Just immerse the blade end in the soup and turn it on, moving it

around the soup until you achieve the desired texture. The solid ingredients must be very soft for the blender to work, and it can never create a completely silken texture. But the immersion blender is still an excellent tool for soups that are only partially pureed, such as some bean soups.

Food Mill (3): Once a soup is cooked until the ingredients are quite soft, the food mill purees and strains simultaneously. Interchangeable disks help the cook control the final texture of the soup. A food mill also strains out tomato seeds.

Making Substitutions

Soups and stews that begin by sautéing vegetables in oil or butter can be adapted by cutting the fat in half and adding ¼ cup water or stock, which sweats the vegetables rather than sautés them. The same vegetables can also be cooked directly in the soup or stew liquid with no previous sautéing at all. Even if you are not concerned about fat, stock should always be degreased before use (see *About Stocks & Broths*, 13) for purely aesthetic reasons. If meat is cooked in a soup or stew, trim it thoroughly; after it has cooked, carefully ladle the fat from the surface—or refrigerate the soup or stew overnight so the fat rises to the top and solidifies, then carefully remove it from the surface.

Most recipes calling for cream can be made with less cream than specified or with none at all, but before you decide against a recipe calling for cream, divide the total amount of cream by the number of servings. Most of the time, a cup of the soup or stew will contain only a few tablespoons of cream. If the soup is not boiled, you can often substitute low-fat milk, yogurt, or a touch of sour cream (which has half the fat of regular cream).

Using Pasta in Soups

Italy's pasta soups fall into two major categories: filled or other pastas cooked in stock and garnished only with grated cheese, and brothy home-style soups with tiny or broken pasta, vegetables, or other flavorful ingredients.

Italian home cooks use whatever is at hand, boiling up broth and dropping into it whatever pasta is handy; by the time the pasta is tender, the vegetables are just right. For more substance, they beat together an egg or two with grated cheese and stir it into the soup about a minute before taking it off the stove.

Tiny pastas are used in several styles of soups: Cook them in the stock and finish the soup with minced fresh herbs and/or grated cheese and/or beaten egg stirred in at the last moment. Add pasta with vegetables or other ingredients for brothy soups.

- Small shapes: meloni, orzo, pastine, tubetti, ditalini, anellini (little rings), stelline, avene (oats), tempestine, and quadrettini.
- Break these long strands into clear soups to whatever size you need: pappardelle, lasagnette, maltagliati, lasagne, bucatini, capellini, vermicelli, spaghetti, and linguine.

STORING SOUPS AND STEWS

Soups and stews keep well, tightly covered in the refrigerator, improving in flavor. The exception is a recipe made with fish and seafood. The delicate flavors of the fish are best as soon as they are cooked. Fruit soups and soups and stews made with meat, poultry, milk, cream, or eggs keep for up to 3 days. Those made of vegetables and legumes keep for up to 4 days.

Refrigerate soup or stew when it has completely cooled and cover tightly. Always store in a container that it completely fills—air is the enemy. For the same reason, be sure to leave any fat on top until serving time, as the layer seals the soup or stew beneath.

All soups and stews can be frozen. Soups that contain chunks of vegetables that do not freeze well—root vegetables, for example—can be pureed after thawing, then heated with enough stock or milk to loosen. Pureed soups hold their quality for up to 3 months in the freezer. Stews and other soups are best served within 1 month of freezing.

SERVING SOUPS AND STEWS

You can serve soup or stew in anything that will hold it, but over the centuries certain bowls have become traditional for certain soups and stews.

First-course soups are usually presented in smaller bowls (**1**) than hearty main-course stews.

Cream soups and consommés, which cool quickly, are traditionally served in comparatively deep bowls (**2**). Occasionally an elegant broth is served in actual demitasse cups and sipped like espresso. The bowls of cream-soup spoons are deep and nearly rounded so that they can hold a reasonable quantity of liquid.

Stews, chowders, fish soups, and other soups with numerous ingredients, which are slower to cool, are usually served in shallow, broad-rimmed dishes (**3**) or in underplates; the appropriate spoons are long-handled and have shallow oval-shaped bowls (**4**) that can hold plenty of chunks.

Use ovenproof bowls or crocks (**5**) for a soup such as French onion, which requires time in the oven.

If you can, serve Asian soups in Chinese or Japanese lacquer or ceramic bowls with those distinctive open-handled ceramic Asian soup spoons (**6**).

As for serving size, consider 1 cup of soup an appetizer, and 1½ to 2 cups of soup or stew a main course.

ABOUT **STOCKS** & BROTHS

*S*tocks and broths are a vital ingredient in many soups and stews, and no store-bought variety can compare with a well-tended homemade version. Stock making is different from other kinds of cooking. Instead of calling for tender, young ingredients, stocks are best made with meat from older animals and mature vegetables, cooked slowly for a long time to extract every vestige of flavor. Purists may insist on using only fish stock in a fish soup or beef stock in a beef stew, but today's household rarely has the luxury of such precision. Since chicken and vegetable stocks are the mildest in flavor and the easiest to prepare, they have become our most popular—and can be used for, among other things, both fish soup and beef stew if necessary. Certainly, full-flavored beef stock or savory white veal stock is still worth making if you have the time.

Clockwise from top: *Vegetable Stock, 20; Chicken Stock, 22; Brown Beef Stock, 24*

Making Stocks and Broths

The characteristics of any good stock are flavor, body, and clarity. Of the three, flavor is paramount, and the way to get it is by using a high proportion of ingredients to water. The most flavorful stocks are made with only enough water to cover the bones, shells, or vegetables. Additional water is needed only when it evaporates below the level of the ingredients before the stock is fully cooked. Follow the recipes for ideal ratios of liquid to solids, but the principle is simple: Keep the solids covered while cooking.

Cooking times for stocks depend on how long it takes to extract all the flavor from the ingredients. While it takes at least 8 hours for raw beef bones to give up all their richness and flavor, chicken bones only need to be boiled for half that time. Vegetable and fish stocks rarely require more than an hour to cook. In fact, their delicate flavors will deteriorate if overcooked. When preparing ingredients for stock making, it is important to chop vegetables and bones to size according to their cooking times—large for long cooking and small for quick cooking—to allow their flavors to be fully extracted.

Simmering the stock past the recipe's recommended cooking time can produce an unpleasant bitter taste. A stock should be strained when all the flavors and goodness have been fully extracted from the meat, bones, and vegetables. If in doubt, retrieve a meaty bone from the simmering stock. If the meat still has some flavor, allow the stock to simmer for longer. If the meat is entirely tasteless and the bone joints are falling apart, it is time to strain the stock.

If a stock tastes weak after straining, remove and discard the fat, then simmer the stock briskly to reduce the water content and concentrate the flavor. This technique, known as reduction and used extensively in sauce making, does produce a more deeply flavored stock, but in the process much of the aromatic, fresh taste of the vegetables is lost. For this reason, we do not recommend reducing vegetable stock. In addition, not all dishes require a deep, concentrated flavor. A light stock is sometimes more appropriate for its subtlety. In instances when you want a hearty stock, first roast the bones and vegetables in a hot oven. Then transfer the bones and vegetables to the stockpot, pour off any excess grease, and add water or wine to the hot roasting pan to release the intensely flavored caramelized cooking juices—a step known as deglazing. Add the liquid to the stockpot. The resulting brown stock is darker and richer than a stock made by straight simmering, which is referred to as a white stock. This technique can be used for meat, poultry, fish, or vegetable stocks.

When choosing meat or bones for the stockpot, understand that meat adds flavor, while bones contribute body. Bones, especially those from the joints (knuckles and shoulders) of young animals, contain gelatin, which gives a stock body and a rich, smooth texture. Always use a combination of bones and meat, or look for particularly meaty bones. By definition, a stock is made with more bones than meat, while a broth is

made from meat. For economy's sake, meat or poultry used for stock making can be removed from the pot before the stock is ready (while the meat still has flavor) and reserved for another meal; see *Express Chicken Broth*, 29. The resulting light stock can be used as is, or the bones can be returned to the pot and the stock cooked further. Raw ingredients produce the best stock, but in a pinch, leftover meat or vegetables will do. Leftover carcasses, such as turkey, broken up and pushed under the water, make a fine stock.

The clarity of a stock is more than an aesthetic concern. A clear stock tastes clean and fresh, while a cloudy one will often seem greasy and muddled. The secret to a clear stock is to start with cold water, allow it to come slowly to a boil, then immediately lower the temperature to the slightest simmer while you carefully skim any impurities, froth, or fat that rises to the surface. This technique not only brings the most flavor out of the ingredients but also draws out impurities in the meat and bones that would otherwise cloud your stock. If a stock is permitted to boil, these impurities, in the form of the scum that forms on the surface of the stock, will be incorporated into the liquid instead. If you do not have enough time to simmer a stock gently, consider preparing one of the express broth recipes in this section. Some are made from scratch, and some call for doctoring already-prepared ingredients. All are time savers.

ADAPTING FLAVOR

If you prefer a lighter soup or a vegetarian soup, any of the all-vegetable stocks, 20, or *Vegetable Broth*, 29, can replace a meat, poultry, fish, or seafood stock in soups and stews. When you need a substitute for beef stock, it is worth your time to prepare *Roasted Vegetable Stock*, 20, which has a similar depth of flavor. Remember that no matter what the soup, a small quantity of salt pork, a ham hock, or a few slices of bacon will add depth in a short time. Use these and other robustly flavored ingredients sparingly. It takes just a little to flavor the pot. Ingredients such as these should not overwhelm the other ingredients, but should be used to enrich flavor.

RULES FOR MAKING STOCKS AND BROTHS

• Cut the ingredients into small pieces for quick-cooking stocks and broths, and larger pieces for long-cooking stocks (**1**). Express broths use the smallest-cut ingredients, followed by fish stock, then vegetable stock, then poultry, and lastly meat.

• The higher the ratio of solids to water, the more flavorful the stock or broth. The water should just barely cover the ingredients (**2**). Add water during cooking if necessary.

• Start with cold water and bring it slowly to a simmer. Never rush a stock. Simmer gently so bubbles just barely break on the surface.

• Never allow a stock to boil.

• Skim the impurities that rise to the surface as the stock or broth simmers—often during the first 30 minutes, and then once an hour or so (**3**). Have two bowls nearby, one filled with water to set the skimmer in so that it does not get covered with congealed fat and impurities, and a second bowl to collect what you skim off.

• Adjust the flavor. If the stock tastes too thin, simmer it until it is flavorful. As the water evaporates, the stock reduces in volume and its flavor is concentrated. Vegetable stock becomes bitter when over-reduced.

• Stop cooking the stock when there is no flavor left in the ingredients.

• A well-made stock or broth contains very little fat. Begin by trimming

all meat and bones of visible fat, and finish by either skimming the stock or broth carefully while still warm or chilling it so the fat forms a solid layer and is easily removed (**4**). Alternatively, and easiest yet, use an inexpensive gravy separator (**5**).

• Many variables affect the yield of a stock or broth recipe, such as the size of the pot and the kind of meat or bones used. Ultimately, a good flavor is more important than achieving the exact yield.

Seasoning Stocks and Broths

Stocks and broths are usually meant to be comparatively unassertive in flavor, so that they can be used for a number of purposes. Onions, carrots, and celery, the traditional mixture of aromatic vegetables for stocks and broths, known as a mirepoix in French, should be added sparingly about 30 minutes after the stock has begun to simmer and the impurities have been removed.

Different styles of cooking alter this classic mixture; in Louisiana, for instance, the standard vegetable mixture includes onions, green peppers, and celery. Mushrooms and leeks are also common. The discreet use of either fresh or dried seasonings, including parsley, thyme, bay leaves, and peppercorns, in the form of a bouquet garni is equally important.

For express broth or quick-cooking stocks, there is no need to tie the seasonings in a bundle—they can simply be tossed in with the vegetables. Salt is almost never added to stocks and broths. The reduction process, during both the original simmering and any subsequent cooking, would concentrate the salt and ruin the results. Vegetable stocks are an exception to the rule. Because they are lighter in flavor and are rarely reduced, some cooks add a small amount of salt during cooking to bring out the flavors.

Court Bouillon

4 cups

Court bouillon is a seasoned liquid cooked for only a short time (court is French for short) and is especially useful when you haven't the time to make an actual stock or when a recipe for soup or stew requires only a lightly flavored broth. The composition of a court bouillon can vary, but most contain some type of acid (lemon juice or wine vinegar) and an assortment of aromatic vegetables and herbs such as parsley, thyme, and bay leaves. Court bouillon and Vegetable Stock, 20, are generally interchangeable, but vegetable stock has no lemon juice or vinegar.

Combine in a stockpot over medium heat:

6 cups cold water
½ cup chopped onions
½ cup chopped celery
¼ cup chopped leeks, tender white part only, washed thoroughly
¼ cup chopped carrots
1 Bouquet Garni, right

Bring to a boil, reduce the heat, and let simmer gently, uncovered, until the vegetables are tender, about 20 minutes. Add:

3 tablespoons lemon juice or white wine vinegar

Simmer for another 10 minutes. Strain into a clean pot or heatproof plastic container. If desired, season with:

Salt and ground black pepper to taste

Use immediately to make soups or stews or let cool, uncovered, then refrigerate until ready to use.

Bouquet Garni

Since herbs tend to float and get in the way as you skim the surface of a stock, we recommend tying them together in a little packet, known as a bouquet garni. Vary the contents to suit your dish, with additions such as whole cloves, dill, lemon zest, or garlic. For express broth or quick-cooking stocks, simply toss the seasonings in with the vegetables.

Wrap in a 4 × 4-inch piece of cheesecloth:

Small bunch of parsley or parsley stems
8 sprigs fresh thyme, or 1 teaspoon dried
1 bay leaf
2 or 3 celery leaves (optional)

Tie the cheesecloth securely with a piece of kitchen string or omit the cheesecloth and simply tie the herbs together at their stems. Refrigerate in a tightly covered container until ready to use.

Reducing Stock to a Glaze

Meat, poultry, and fish (but not vegetable) stocks can be cooked down, or reduced, until they become a thick, syrupy glaze that is both potent and delectable. Although the lengthy reduction takes patience and care, the end product becomes a wonderfully convenient "secret ingredient" for seasoning and finishing all manner of soups and stews. When it is fully reduced, a glaze is just 10 to 15 percent of the volume of original stock and will last for months tightly covered in the refrigerator. Reduced fish stock tends to be too strong for most tastes.
Prepare:

4 cups *Brown Beef Stock, 24, Brown Veal Stock, 25, or Brown Chicken Stock, 22*

Degrease the stock well and place it in a large pot over medium-high heat. Allow the stock to simmer vigorously. Skim any foam that rises to the surface and transfer the stock to gradually smaller pots as it reduces in volume. Lower the heat when the stock begins to get noticeably thicker and more concentrated to avoid burning. The glaze is ready when it coats the back of a spoon and only about 1 cup remains, anywhere from 2 to 4 hours depending on the shape of the pan.

Remove from the heat and let cool. The glaze will solidify and feel rubbery to the touch. Cover and refrigerate, or cut into small squares equivalent to 1 tablespoon or more and freeze for use in preparing soups or stews.

IS STOCK NECESSARY?

It depends on the soup or stew. Some need stock for taste and body. *French Onion Soup, 53,* derives its rich color and deep flavor from beef stock. Similarly, most single-vegetable soups need the depth of flavor that a savory liquid brings. In some cases, stock is the very soul of the soup: *Matzo Ball Soup, 33,* is really chicken stock with matzo balls in it.

But when the main ingredients of a soup or stew are full of character, you may not want to mask their flavors by adding stock. The beets in *New York Deli Borscht, 48,* the vegetables in *Provençal Vegetable Soup, 59,* the meat in *Oxtail Soup, 104,* need nothing more than water to carry their powerful flavors. Likewise, most soups and stews based on beans and legumes, 65 to 72, do not require stock, their main ingredients being rich and earthy. Keep in mind that a few soups and stews can be prepared either with stock or without. *Minestrone, 46,* may have a warmer flavor with chicken stock, but it is also fine with water.

A classic stock—composed of many ingredients, simmered for hours, strained, and reduced—is essential only for soups and stews where the broth is the main component. For most other recipes, an express broth, 28 to 29, will work perfectly well. So will a canned stock. Low-sodium canned stocks are preferable, because the lack of salt leaves the cook freer to adjust the seasonings.

HOW TO STRAIN AND STORE STOCK

1 When the stock has finished cooking, strain it through a fine-mesh sieve (or a colander lined with a double layer of cheesecloth or a coffee filter) into another pot or a large heatproof container and discard the solids.

2 Pressing heavily on the solids while straining may cloud the stock. We have recommended it for the vegetable stock recipes, where the extra flavor from the cooked vegetables is needed.

3 Do not let the stock sit out at room temperature for long as it is a good breeding ground for bacteria. Speed up the cooling process by placing the hot bowl, uncovered, in another bowl of ice water and stirring it a few times.

4 Once the stock cools enough so that it will not raise the temperature of your refrigerator, cover it tightly and chill it. When the stock is chilled, any fat will rise in a solid mass that must be removed before reheating. While cold, this fat layer (shown on chicken stock) actually protects the stock.

5 Stock will keep for 3 to 5 days in the refrigerator. If refrigerated for longer, after 3 days skim the solidified fat from the surface and boil the stock for 10 minutes, then refrigerate it for another 3 to 5 days.

6 For prolonged storage, transfer stock to pint or quart plastic containers or plastic freezer bags and freeze it. Small amounts of stock can also be frozen in ice cube trays. See also *Reducing Stock to a Glaze, opposite,* for other storage possibilities.

Vegetable Stock

About 4 cups

Vegetable stocks allow for much improvisation. Good additions include onions, carrots, potatoes, corncobs, fennel, fresh herbs, ginger, garlic, washed organic vegetable skins, and even a few tablespoons of lentils. Vegetables to avoid include those in the cabbage family (except when used deliberately and with discretion), eggplant, and most strong greens (with the exception of kale); too many carrots or parsnips will turn the stock overly sweet. When possible, tailor the ingredients to suit the recipe the stock will be used in. For example, a stock accented with ginger and garlic would be good in many Asian recipes.

Combine in a stockpot:

1 medium onion, sliced
1 leek, white part only, cleaned thoroughly and sliced
1 carrot, peeled and sliced
1 small turnip, peeled and sliced
6 cloves garlic, peeled and smashed
6 cups cold water
1 *Bouquet Garni*, 17

Simmer gently, partially covered, until the vegetables are completely softened, 45 to 60 minutes. Strain into a clean pot or heatproof plastic container, pressing down on the vegetables to extract the juices. Season with:

Salt and ground black pepper to taste (optional)

Let cool, uncovered, then refrigerate until ready to use.

Roasted Vegetable Stock

About 4 cups

Preheat the oven to 400°F. Lightly grease a roasting pan.

Toss together in the prepared pan and roast, stirring occasionally, until well browned, about 1 hour:

8 ounces mushrooms or mushroom stems, wiped clean
1 onion, quartered
2 carrots, peeled and cut into 2-inch pieces
8 cloves garlic, peeled and smashed
1 small turnip, peeled and cut into 2-inch pieces

Remove the vegetables to a stockpot, then deglaze the hot roasting pan by adding:

1 cup cold water

Scrape up any browned bits, then add the liquid to the pot along with:

6 cups cold water
1 *Bouquet Garni*, 17, including a pinch of red pepper flakes

Simmer gently, uncovered, until the vegetables are completely softened, 45 to 60 minutes. Strain into a clean pot or heatproof plastic container, pressing down on the vegetables to extract the juices. Season with:

Salt to taste

Let cool, uncovered, then refrigerate until ready to use.

Shrimp Stock

About 3 cups

For a clear stock, omit the tomato paste.

Heat in a stockpot over medium-high heat:

2 tablespoons vegetable oil

Add and cook, stirring occasionally, until the shells are bright pink and aromatic, about 15 minutes:

3 cups uncooked shrimp shells, well rinsed and drained (from about 2 pounds shrimp)

2 small onions, diced
2 small carrots, peeled and diced
2 celery stalks, diced

Stir in:

2 tablespoons tomato paste (optional)

Add:

6 cups cold water
1 bay leaf
1½ teaspoons lightly crushed black peppercorns

Splash of Pernod or ¼ teaspoon fennel seeds (optional)

Bring almost to a boil, reduce the heat, and simmer gently, partially covered, for 20 minutes. Strain into a clean pot or heatproof plastic container, pressing down on the shells to extract all the liquid. Let cool, uncovered, then refrigerate until ready to use.

Fish Stock

About 6 cups

If fish bones are unavailable, use inexpensive whole fish. For a mild-tasting, all-purpose fish stock, avoid oily fish.

Combine in a stockpot over medium heat:

2 pounds fish heads and bones, or whole fish, scaled, gutted, gills and viscera removed, rinsed well and drained
1 small onion, sliced
1 large leek, white and tender green parts, cleaned thoroughly and sliced
½ fennel bulb, sliced (optional)

1 to 2 cloves garlic (optional)
1 cup dry white wine (optional)
6 cups cold water (or just enough to cover)
1 *Bouquet Garni, 17*

Bring to a boil, reduce the heat, and simmer gently. Cook, uncovered, skimming often, for 30 to 40 minutes. Strain into a clean pot or heatproof plastic container. Let cool, uncovered, then refrigerate until ready to use.

FISH FUMET

Prepare *Fish Stock, left*, first cooking the vegetables over medium-low heat in 2 tablespoons butter until they begin to soften, about 5 minutes. Add the fish heads and bones and cook, stirring once or twice, until they begin to turn opaque, 5 minutes more. Be sure not to let the vegetables or fish brown. Add the wine, cold water, and bouquet garni and continue as directed.

BAY LAUREL LEAVES AND PEPPERCORNS

From a graceful evergreen tree, bay laurel leaves are long, narrow, pointed, dark, and leathery. Their flavor is pungent and complex—something between eucalyptus, mint, lemon, and fresh-cut grass. Do not confuse them with the far commoner California bay, which is what is sold in this country as "bay leaves." European bay laurel leaves are labeled as imported.

Pepper berries are the fruit of a leafy green vine that has spikes of white flowers; the flowers become clusters of green berries. These green peppercorns have a mild fresh flavor. Black peppercorns are green berries that are piled up and fermented for a few days, then dried in the sun, to become hard, wrinkled, and dark brown to black. Their flavor is rich and spicy, especially if the

berries are Malabar peppercorns. Used whole to flavor soups and stews, the flavor of peppercorns is discreet; tie the whole berries in a piece of cheesecloth, then remove them before serving. When peppercorns are freshly crushed with a mortar and pestle, most of their oils are retained and the flavor is enormously pungent.

Chicken Stock

About 8 cups

Using the lesser amount of chicken suggested here, will result in a lighter stock (opposite), which will reinforce the flavor in many dishes without adding a pronounced chicken taste; the greater amount will yield a richer one.

Combine in a stockpot over medium heat:

4 to 5½ pounds chicken parts (backs, necks, wings, legs, or thighs), or 1 whole 4- to 5½-pound roasting chicken, well rinsed

16 cups cold water (or just enough to cover)

Bring to a boil, reduce the heat, and simmer gently. Skim often until impurities no longer appear, about 30 minutes. Add:

1 onion, coarsely chopped

1 carrot, peeled and coarsely chopped

1 celery stalk, coarsely chopped

1 *Bouquet Garni*, 17

Simmer, uncovered, for 3 hours, adding water as needed to cover. Strain into a clean pot or heatproof plastic container. Let cool, uncovered, then refrigerate. Remove the fat when ready to use.

BROWN (OR ROASTED) CHICKEN STOCK

This chicken stock variation has a richer flavor than "white" chicken stock. It can be used for hearty chicken soups and stews or in place of beef stock. Preheat the oven to 425°F. Prepare *Chicken Stock, above,* first combining the chicken parts and vegetables, without the bouquet garni, in a heavy roasting pan and roasting, stirring occasionally, until well browned, about 1 hour. Remove the chicken and vegetables to a stockpot and deglaze the hot roasting pan by adding 1 cup water and scraping up any browned bits. Add the liquid to the pot along with water to cover, about 16 cups, and the bouquet garni. Continue as directed.

COOKING ONIONS

Cooking onions are the common medium to large yellow, red, and white onions that never fail us at the market. Skin color has less to do with the flavor of a cooking onion than its variety and where it was grown. Generally, yellow onions are richly flavored but on the sharp side when raw. Most sweeten when carefully cooked. White onions are often pungent when raw, but there are mild varieties like White Sweet Spanish. In some parts of the country, Spanish is understood to mean a very large, mild, yellow onion. Breeders can attach the word *Spanish* to mild onions of every size and color. Red onions are usually on the sweet side and can be cooked the same way but do not store as well as most yellow and white onions. Cooking onions of all kinds should be tightly closed and very firm, without soft spots or black, powdery patches of mold. To store dried onions, spread them out—do not heap—in a cool, dry place. Wrap cut onions tightly in plastic wrap and refrigerate in the vegetable crisper.

Turkey Stock

12 to 20 cups

This stock is the perfect use for a leftover Thanksgiving turkey carcass and the accompanying bits of meat. If the carcass is very large, break it into pieces before adding it to the pot. Turkey stock can be substituted in any dish calling for chicken stock.

Barely cover with cold water in a large stockpot over medium heat:

1 meaty turkey carcass, from a 12- to 25-pound turkey, broken up

Bring to a boil, reduce the heat, and simmer gently. Skim often until impurities no longer appear, about 30 minutes. Add:

1 onion, quartered

1 carrot, peeled and cut into 1-inch pieces

1 celery stalk, cut into 1-inch pieces

1 *Bouquet Garni*, 17

Simmer, uncovered, for 3 hours. Skim any impurities that rise and add water as needed to cover. Strain into a clean pot or heatproof plastic container. Let cool, uncovered, then refrigerate. Remove the fat when ready to use.

Brown Beef Stock

About 10 cups

The combination of beef shanks and chicken bones produces a hearty stock in half the time it takes to make Classic Beef Stock, right.

Preheat the oven to 425°F. Lightly oil a roasting pan. Place in the prepared pan and roast for 15 minutes:

3 pounds meaty beef shanks, cut into 2-inch pieces, or oxtails, split into chunks, or a combination

Add:

1 pound chicken parts (backs, necks, wings, legs, or thighs), well rinsed

2 medium onions, quartered

2 carrots, peeled and thickly sliced

2 celery stalks, cut into 2-inch pieces

Roast, stirring occasionally to prevent the vegetables from burning, until the bones are well browned, about 40 minutes. Transfer the meat and vegetables to a stockpot, carefully pour off any excess grease without discarding the caramelized cooking juices, and add to the hot roasting pan:

2 cups cold water

Scrape up any browned bits, then add the liquid to the pot along with:

14 cups cold water (or just enough to cover)

Bring to a boil over medium heat, skim off the impurities, reduce the heat, and simmer gently. Skim often until impurities no longer appear, about 30 minutes. Add:

1 leek, split lengthwise, cleaned thoroughly, and cut into 2-inch pieces

1 *Bouquet Garni*, 17, including 1 whole clove

Simmer, uncovered, for 4 hours, skimming as necessary and adding water as needed to cover. Strain into a clean pot or heatproof plastic container. Let cool, uncovered, then refrigerate. Remove the fat when ready to use.

CLASSIC BEEF STOCK

Prepare *Brown Beef Stock, left*, substituting 5 pounds beef bones, preferably knucklebones, for the beef shanks and chicken. Cut the vegetables into larger pieces and simmer the stock for 8 hours.

LAMB STOCK

About 7 cups

Lamb Stock (below) boosts the flavor of lamb soups and stews. Do not use it in recipes calling for fowl or other kinds of meat. Its flavor can be assertive and could easily overpower more delicate foods. Prepare Brown Beef Stock, left, substituting 2 pounds lamb shoulder chops, well trimmed, for the beef and chicken and decreasing the onions, carrots, celery, and water by one-half. Omit the leek. Simmer for 3 hours.

Game Stock

About 8 cups

This stock can be made with rabbit or with duck, guinea hen, or other small game birds.

Combine in a stockpot over medium heat:

One 3-pound rabbit or fowl, or 3 pounds meaty game bones, rinsed and drained

16 cups cold water

Bring to a boil, reduce the heat, and simmer gently. Skim often until impurities no longer appear, about 30 minutes.

Add:

1 medium onion, coarsely chopped

1 carrot, peeled and cut into 1-inch pieces

1 celery stalk, cut into 1-inch pieces

1 *Bouquet Garni*, 17

Simmer, uncovered, for 2½ hours, adding water as needed to cover. Strain into a clean pot or heatproof plastic container. Let cool, uncovered, then refrigerate. Remove the fat when ready to use.

White Veal Stock

About 8 cups

The comparatively mild flavor of this stock makes it highly versatile. Blanching the veal breast and bones by briefly boiling them and discarding the water helps create a clear stock. Ask your butcher to split the veal bones.

Cover with cold water in a stockpot over high heat:

1½ pounds veal breast
1½ pounds veal knucklebones, split

Bring to a boil. Immediately drain and rinse the veal, the bones, and the pot. Return the veal breast and bones to the pot along with:

12 ounces chicken parts (backs, necks, wings, legs, or thighs), well rinsed
12 cups cold water (or just enough to cover)

Bring to a boil, skim off the impurities, and reduce the heat. Simmer gently for about 20 minutes. Add:

2 large onions, coarsely chopped
2 medium leeks, white and tender green parts, cleaned thoroughly and chopped
2 carrots, peeled and coarsely chopped
1 celery stalk, coarsely chopped
1 *Bouquet Garni*, 17

Simmer, uncovered, for 3 to 4 hours, adding water as needed to cover. Strain into a clean pot or heatproof plastic container. Let cool, uncovered, then refrigerate. Remove the fat when ready to use.

BROWN VEAL STOCK

Preheat the oven to 425°F. Lightly grease a roasting pan. Proceed as for *White Veal Stock*, left, but first roast the veal breast and bones in the prepared pan for 15 minutes; add the chicken and vegetables and roast until well browned, about 1 hour. Remove the meat and vegetables to a stockpot, carefully pour off any excess grease without discarding the caramelized cooking juices, and add 1 cup cold water or wine (red or white) to the hot roasting pan. Scrape up any browned bits, then add the liquid to the pot along with cold water to cover. Bring to a boil, reduce the heat, and simmer gently, skimming often for the first 30 minutes. Add the bouquet garni and continue as directed.

Dashi

About 4 cups

One of the bases of traditional Japanese cuisine, this stock is made quickly, from just two ingredients— kombu, or kelp, and katsuobushi, or dried bonito flakes, also referred to as smoky fish flakes—both of which can be found in Asian markets or health food stores. Dashi should be used within 4 to 5 days of preparation.

It should not be boiled or cooked for too long, and it does not freeze well. When reheating, do not boil.

Combine in a stockpot over high heat:

One 5 x 4-inch piece kombu (kelp)

4½ cups cold water

Bring almost to a boil. Immediately remove from the heat and stir in:

⅓ cup loosely packed *katsuobushi* (dried bonito flakes)

Let stand until the flakes begin to sink, 2 to 3 minutes (opposite). Remove the kombu with tongs. Strain the stock at once into a clean pot or heatproof plastic container. Let cool, uncovered, then refrigerate until ready to use.

Chicken-Enriched Dashi (Tori-Gara Dashi)

About 4 cups

Cover with cold water in a stockpot over high heat:

1 pound chicken parts (backs, necks, wings, legs, or thighs), well rinsed

Bring to a boil. Immediately drain and rinse the chicken parts and the pot. Return the chicken to the pot along with:

One 5 x 4-inch piece kombu (kelp)

6 cups cold water

Bring to a boil, reduce the heat, and simmer gently. Cook, uncovered, skimming often, for 20 to 25 minutes. Season with:

1 tablespoon light or dark soy sauce

Remove from the heat and stir in:

⅓ cup loosely packed *katsuobushi* (dried bonito flakes)

Let stand until the flakes begin to sink, 2 to 3 minutes. Remove the kombu with tongs. Strain the stock into a clean pot or heatproof plastic container. Let cool, uncovered, then refrigerate until ready to use.

KELP AND BONITO FLAKES

Sold as "Dashi Kombu," a 6-ounce package of kelp is enough to make six batches of broth for 4 to 6 people. The whitish coating on kelp is natural. Kelp should never be washed, or it will lose flavor. Kelp keeps indefinitely if it is stored tightly sealed.

Bonito flakes are dried, salted, fermented fish flakes. Bonito flakes will keep indefinitely on a cool, dark shelf in the pantry.

CHIPOTLE PEPPER

Chipotle peppers (dried smoked jalapeños) have made great gains in popularity in this country for their intense, rich, smoky flavor. These days they show up everywhere, from canned tomato sauce (adobo) to stews, soups, salsas, sauces, pickles, and more. There are two types of chipotles, both made from different cultivars of the jalapeño. The first is the black-red chili chipotle (also known as the chipotle colorado, mora, or morita); this small chipotle (1 to 1½ inches long and ½ inch wide) is prized for its sweet, smoked flavor and its dark, rosewood red color. The second type, usually called chipotle meco, is larger (3 to 4 inches long by 1 inch wide) and pale brown in color, with a more tobacco-like taste and usually less heat.

About Broths

Unlike stocks, which are made primarily from bones, broths are made from meat (except for vegetable broth), and they cook for shorter periods of time. The resulting liquid has a fresher, more definable flavor but less body than a stock. For this reason, broths are ideal for soups. Most of the canned stocks sold today are closer to broths and are best used in soups, not sauces, since they are often seasoned with salt and other seasonings, which makes it inadvisable to boil them down.

Express Fish Broth

About 4 cups

When you haven't the time or inclination to procure fish bones for fish stock, the combination of bottled clam juice and canned chicken broth or stock provides a decent substitute. If you have any fish trimmings on hand, throw them in as well.
Heat in a medium, heavy skillet:
1½ teaspoons olive oil
Add:
1 carrot, peeled and finely chopped
1 small onion or large leek, finely chopped
1 clove garlic, finely chopped
Cook, stirring, over medium-high heat until soft. Add:
½ cup dry vermouth
Stir for about 1 minute, then blend in:
Four 8-ounce bottles clam juice
1½ cups mild chicken broth
Any fish trimmings on hand (optional)
¼ small lemon (optional)
Simmer for 20 minutes, skimming and stirring occasionally. Strain into a clean pot or heatproof plastic container. Let cool, uncovered, then refrigerate until ready to use.

Express Shellfish Chipotle Broth

About 2½ cups

This light but highly flavorful broth is good enough to be used as a sauce. Ladle an ounce or two over vegetables, legumes, or seafood immediately before serving.
Combine in a large saucepan over medium heat:
1½ cups uncooked shrimp shells, well rinsed and drained (from about 1 pound shrimp)
2 teaspoons tomato paste
½ teaspoon chopped chipotle peppers in adobo sauce, or to taste
Large pinch of saffron
½ cup dry white wine
Bring almost to a boil, reduce the heat, and simmer gently, partially covered, for 5 to 10 minutes. Add:
2½ cups *Chicken Stock*, 22
Simmer for 10 minutes more. Strain through a fine-mesh sieve and let the stock rest for a few minutes to allow any solids to settle. Carefully transfer to a clean saucepan or heatproof plastic container, leaving the solids behind. Use immediately or let cool, uncovered, then refrigerate until ready to use.

Chicken Broth

About 12 cups

Once this broth is made, the chicken can be removed and used in soup or other dishes calling for cooked chicken.
Combine in a stockpot over medium heat:

1 whole 3½- to 4-pound chicken, well rinsed
12 cups cold water
Bring almost to a boil, reduce the heat, and simmer gently, skimming often until impurities no longer appear. Meanwhile, pulse in a food processor until finely chopped:

1 medium onion, cut into eighths
1 carrot, peeled and cut into 2-inch pieces
1 celery stalk, cut into 2-inch pieces

Add the chopped vegetables to the pot. Simmer, uncovered, until the chicken is cooked, about 40 minutes. Remove the chicken and reserve. Strain the broth into a clean pot or heatproof plastic container. Let cool, uncovered, then refrigerate. Remove the fat when ready to use.

Express Chicken Broth

About 4 cups

This broth can also be made with canned beef broth or consommé; just omit the giblets.
Combine in a heavy saucepan:

Three 14½-ounce cans ready-to-serve reduced-sodium chicken broth
Any chicken giblets, trimmings, or bones on hand (optional)

Contents of 1 *Bouquet Garni*, 17 (no need to wrap)
Cut into 1-inch pieces and pulse in a food processor until finely chopped:

1 small onion
1 small carrot
1 small celery stalk, with leaves
1 leek, white part only, cleaned thoroughly, or 3 whole scallions

1 small clove garlic (optional)
Bring almost to a boil over medium-high heat, reduce the heat, and simmer gently for about 30 minutes. Strain into a clean pot or heatproof plastic container. Let cool, uncovered, then refrigerate. Remove the fat when ready to use.

Express Beef Broth

About 4 cups

This broth has a good, beefy flavor.
Combine in a stockpot over medium heat:

1½ pounds boneless beef chuck, cut into 1-inch cubes and pulsed in a food processor until coarsely chopped
5 cups cold water
Bring almost to a boil, reduce the heat, and simmer gently, skimming often until impurities no longer appear. Add:

1 onion, cut into 1-inch pieces
1 large leek, white and tender green parts, cleaned thoroughly and chopped

1 carrot, peeled and sliced
1 tablespoon tomato paste
5 parsley stems
½ teaspoon dried thyme
3 black peppercorns, lightly crushed
1 whole clove
Simmer, uncovered, for 1 hour. Strain into a clean pot or heatproof plastic container. Let cool, uncovered, then refrigerate. Remove the fat when ready to use. The stock will separate, so whisk before using.

VEGETABLE BROTH

Use this method to extract the most flavor from the vegetables. Cooking the vegetables before adding them to the stockpot helps to express their flavor. This broth may not need to simmer as long as Vegetable Stock. Prepare Vegetable Stock, 20, first cooking the vegetables over medium heat in 2 tablespoons unsalted butter or oil, stirring occasionally, until they are wilted, about 15 minutes. Add the water and seasonings and continue as directed.

ABOUT
CLEAR STOCKS
WITH ADDITIONS

*T*his is one category of soups for which a tasty, full-bodied home-made stock is strongly recommended. You can intensify the flavor of a light stock by simmering it to evaporate some of the water. Or simmer it with chopped vegetables—finely diced carrots, celery, and onions—and perhaps fresh herbs, then strain out the vegetables. The ultimate broth is consommé, 32, enriched with both meat and vegetables and clarified with egg whites.

Many of the recipes in this section call for chicken stock, because it is easy to prepare and seems to have the most universal appeal. Feel free to substitute any of the stocks provided in About Stocks & Broths, 13.

Chicken Noodle Soup, 33

Chicken or Beef Consommé

About 6½ cups

Clear, intensely flavorful consommé, one of the glories of classical French cooking, makes an elegant start to a formal dinner party. For a clear consommé, the stock must be completely free of grease. For particularly strong consommé, simmer 16 cups (4 quarts) of degreased stock until reduced by half before clarifying it.

Combine in a food processor:

1 small onion, quartered

1 small carrot, peeled and cut into 2-inch pieces

1 small celery stalk, cut into 2-inch pieces

2 tablespoons packed fresh parsley leaves

½ teaspoon fresh thyme leaves

Pulse until coarsely chopped. Add:

1 pound boneless, skinless chicken breasts, fat trimmed, cut into 2-inch pieces, or 1½ pounds beef round or rump steak, fat trimmed, cut into 1-inch pieces

Pulse until chopped but not pureed.

Remove to a medium bowl. Add:

3 large egg whites

Stir together well. Warm in a soup pot, over low heat:

8 cups *Chicken Stock*, 22, *Classic Beef Stock*, 24, or *Brown Beef Stock*, 24, thoroughly degreased

Whisk in the vegetable mixture. Very slowly bring to a simmer without boiling, occasionally stirring and scraping the bottom of the pot to prevent burning until the egg foam rises to the surface, about 30 minutes. (Be careful not to stir after the broth reaches a simmer.) When the egg foam starts to solidify, make a small hole in the center with the end of a wooden spoon. Continue to simmer very gently until the egg foam mixture is solid, about 30 minutes more. Remove the pot from the heat. Line a sieve with a slightly dampened cheesecloth or dish towel. Gently move the foam to the side of the pot and ladle out the consommé. Strain the consommé through the sieve into a large saucepan. Season with:

1 teaspoon salt, or to taste

Heat through, then ladle into warmed bowls.

CONSOMMÉ BRUNOISE

In classical French cooking, a brunoise is a mixture of finely diced vegetables. This recipe uses three vegetables most basic to the French kitchen. Prepare Chicken or Beef Consommé, above, adding with the salt: 2 tablespoons very finely diced leeks (white part only), 2 tablespoons very finely diced carrots, and 2 tablespoons very finely diced celery. Simmer gently until the vegetables are tender, about 5 minutes. Ladle into warmed bowls.

Chicken Noodle Soup

About 4 cups

Using homemade stock in this recipe makes all the difference, transforming a dependable standard into a great soup. If you do make your own stock, remove some of the chicken meat from the bones when the stock is done and return it to the soup. For variety, try stirring in a peeled, seeded, and diced tomato and a teaspoon of chopped fresh herb, such as tarragon, parsley, dill, or basil, just before serving the soup.

Bring to a boil in a medium saucepan:

4 cups Chicken Stock, 22, or Brown Chicken Stock, 22

Stir in:

1 cup fine egg noodles or 2 ounces thin fresh or dried pasta

Cook until the pasta is tender but firm, 4 to 5 minutes. Season with:

2 tablespoons chopped fresh parsley
Salt to taste
Pinch of ground black pepper

Ladle into warmed bowls.

Chicken Rice or Barley Soup

About 4 cups

With simple additions, flavorful home-made chicken stock can be transformed into a multitude of other soups. (Vegetarians can substitute Vegetable Stock, 20.) If you are adding grains and vegetables, add the vegetables when the grains are almost cooked.

Bring to a simmer in a medium saucepan:

4 cups Chicken Stock, 22, or Brown Chicken Stock, 22
½ teaspoon salt

Stir in:

3 tablespoons long-grain rice or 2 tablespoons pearl barley

Simmer until tender, about 15 minutes for rice, 30 to 45 minutes for barley.

Chicken Soup with Ravioli or Tortellini

Prepare Chicken Rice or Barley Soup, left, substituting ravioli or tortellini (quantity to taste) for the rice or barley. Simmer until tender but firm, 5 to 10 minutes. Any of the following can be added to or substituted for the additions above:

Stir in 5 minutes before the soup is fully cooked:

1½ cups sliced mixed vegetables, such as carrots, celery, tomatoes, and/or onions

Stir in 1 to 2 minutes before the soup is fully cooked:

1 cup thinly sliced greens (such as escarole, kale, or spinach), trimmed, washed, and dried

Stir in any of the following just before serving:

1 tablespoon dry sherry
Chopped basil or parsley
Pinch of ground black pepper

Matzo Ball Soup

About 6 cups; 12 to 14 large balls

This simple classic is wonderful with or without the optional additions.

Beat on medium speed for 1 minute:

4 large eggs
1 teaspoon salt

If desired, stir in:

½ cup finely diced fennel; 2 tablespoons snipped fresh dill and 4 teaspoons snipped fresh or dried chives; or 2 tablespoons chopped fresh parsley and 2 tablespoons snipped fresh dill (optional)

Stir in:

⅓ cup plus 1 tablespoon soda water

Fold in until well blended:

1 cup matzo meal
¼ teaspoon ground black pepper
1 teaspoon curry powder (optional)
1 to 2 teaspoons finely chopped peeled fresh ginger, or 1 teaspoon ground (optional)

Cover and refrigerate for 1 to 4 hours. With wet hands, form the matzo balls. Drop the balls into a large pot of boiling salted water, cover, reduce the heat, and simmer for 20 minutes. When the matzo balls are almost finished, heat in a soup pot:

6 cups Chicken Stock, 22

Season with:

1¼ teaspoons salt
¼ teaspoon ground black pepper (optional)

When the matzo balls are finished, add them to the stock. Ladle the stock into warmed bowls and add 2 matzo balls to each serving.

Chinese Egg Drop Soup

About 4 cups

A simple, delicate soup.
Combine in a large saucepan and simmer, partially covered, for 15 minutes:

4 cups Chicken Stock, *22*
2 large slices fresh ginger
2 large cloves garlic, smashed and peeled

Discard the ginger and garlic. Stir together in a small bowl:

1 tablespoon cornstarch
3 tablespoons water

Bring the soup to a low simmer and add the cornstarch mixture. Stir until the soup is slightly thickened. Stir in:

1 teaspoon salt
⅛ teaspoon ground black pepper

Whisk together thoroughly in a small bowl:

1 large egg

1 teaspoon vegetable oil

Bring the soup to a very low simmer and pour the egg mixture in a large circle on the surface of the soup. Once the egg sets, stir gently. Stir in:

2 scallions, diagonally sliced
2 tablespoons chopped fresh cilantro

Ladle into warmed bowls.

Italian Parmesan and Egg Soup (Stracciatella)

About 3 cups

A Roman specialty, stracciatella *derives its name from the word* straccetti, *little rags—describing the strands of cooked egg that float in the broth.*

Bring to a simmer in a medium saucepan:

3 cups Chicken Stock, 22

Meanwhile, whisk together in a small bowl until well blended:

1 large egg

1½ tablespoons grated Parmesan cheese

1 tablespoon dry unseasoned breadcrumbs

2 tablespoons chopped fresh parsley

1 small clove garlic, finely minced

Stir this mixture rapidly into the simmering stock and stir until the egg is set, 30 to 60 seconds.

Garnish with:

Freshly grated or ground nutmeg or grated lemon zest

Ladle into warmed bowls.

Greek Lemon Soup

About 4 cups

Unlike stracciatella, *where the eggs are supposed to separate, here the eggs are blended to create a smooth, creamy texture. This is done by adding a little of the hot stock to the eggs before they are added to the soup to prevent them from curdling.*

Bring to a rolling boil in a medium saucepan:

3 cups Chicken Stock, 22

½ cup long-grain rice

Reduce the heat, cover, and simmer until the rice is tender, about 20 minutes. In a medium bowl, whisk just enough to combine and be uniform in color:

2 large eggs

¼ cup fresh lemon juice

Stir 2 tablespoons of the hot stock into the egg mixture. To prevent curdling, gradually pour the egg mixture into the hot, not boiling, soup while stirring constantly.

Season with:

1 to 2 tablespoons fresh lemon juice (optional)

Salt and ground black pepper to taste

Ladle into warmed bowls.

Garnish with:

Chopped fresh parsley or snipped fresh dill

Miso and Miso Soups

Miso, a fermented paste made from soybeans, comes in a variety of colors (from white to yellow to red) and textures (smooth or chunky), depending on the length of fermentation and the addition of grains such as barley or rice. As a general rule, the darker the miso, the longer it has been fermented and the stronger and saltier it will taste. Lighter miso, fermented for a shorter period, is sweeter. Barley miso is earthy and well aged. Although miso rarely spoils, it loses its flavor after a few months. Keep opened containers in the refrigerator.

Miso soups are an essential part of the traditional Japanese breakfast, though soups thickened with miso also appear at lunch and dinner. In Japan, there are many varieties of miso. Here are two basic miso soups, one based on the light-colored, mellow miso that is popular in Kyoto and Osaka, and the other a dark-colored, pungent red miso that is favored in the region of Tokyo.

Dark-Colored Miso Soup with Sautéed Vegetables

About 4½ cups

This is a rich and flavorful miso soup.
Soak in cold water for 10 minutes:

1½ teaspoons dried *wakame* bits (optional)

Drain, squeeze out the excess liquid, and divide the *wakame* among 4 soup bowls. Heat in a medium saucepan over high heat:

1 teaspoon vegetable oil

Add and cook, stirring, until slightly browned, about 1 minute:

2 to 3 fresh shiitake mushroom caps, thinly sliced
1 small leek (white part only), cleaned thoroughly and thinly sliced on a diagonal

Add:

Pinch of salt
½ teaspoon sake (optional)

Cook, stirring, until the leeks are wilted, about another minute. Stir in:

4 cups *Dashi*, 27

1 teaspoon light or dark soy sauce

Cook over medium-low heat until warm. Place in a small bowl:

3 to 3½ tablespoons red miso

Add about ¼ cup of the warm dashi and whisk to dissolve the miso; then whisk this mixture back into the soup. Ladle the hot miso-thickened broth and vegetables over the *wakame*.
Serve immediately.

WAKAME

Wakame is an edible seaweed. After the leaves of the plant have been soaked, they are briefly cooked in soups or can be used to make a salad. *Wakame* makes a nice addition to miso soups. *Wakame* is sold dried and packaged, sometimes labeled *ito-wakame*. To reconstitute dried *wakame*, simply soak it in tepid water for 20 minutes, to maintain its flavor and the seaweed's high nutritional value. If the stem of the seaweed is present, it should be discarded.

Light-Colored Miso Soup with Simmered Vegetables

About 4½ cups

Autumn brings enormous (foot-long) pure white, carrot-shaped, juicy radishes called daikon *in Japan. These radishes are mild in flavor and often added to soups.*

Bring to a simmer in a medium saucepan:

4 cups Dashi, 27

Season with:

1 teaspoon light or dark soy sauce
Splash of sake (optional)

Stir in and simmer until barely tender, 2 to 3 minutes:

1 small carrot, peeled, halved lengthwise, and thinly sliced
One 2-inch piece daikon radish, peeled, halved lengthwise, and thinly sliced

Place in a small bowl:

3 tablespoons light-colored miso, such as shiro mugi miso (barley-enriched miso)

Add about ¼ cup of the warm dashi and whisk to dissolve the miso; then whisk this mixture back into the soup. Divide among 4 bowls:

1 small scallion, chopped
2 ounces firm tofu, cut into small cubes

Ladle the hot miso-thickened broth and vegetables into the bowls. Serve immediately.

Mongolian Hot Pot

About 8 cups; 6 to 8 servings

A hot pot is a round basin with a sort of chimney in the middle containing smoldering coals to heat stock, shown below. This device can be found in Asian shops or specialty cookware stores, but a fondue pot or electric skillet, while not as dramatic, can easily be substituted. In China, diners cook their own meat and vegetables in the sizzlingly hot stock, then dip them into a sauce they assemble from a selection of seasonings set out on the table. When all the meat and vegetables have been eaten, the guests sip the remaining soup. This is a wonderful party dish. The meat is easier to slice thinly if frozen for 20 minutes first.

For the dipping sauce, puree in a blender:

½ cup rice vinegar
⅓ cup sugar or ¼ cup honey
½ cup light or dark soy sauce
⅓ cup red miso or rinsed
   fermented black beans
¼ cup toasted sesame oil
1 tablespoon minced peeled
   fresh ginger
2 teaspoons chili oil, or more
   to taste
3 cloves garlic, chopped

Pour the sauce into individual serving bowls and garnish with:

Chopped scallions (about
   3 scallions)
Chopped fresh cilantro
Snipped fresh chives

Arrange decoratively on a platter:

2 pounds beef sirloin steak or lamb
   loin, fat trimmed, thinly sliced
3 cups sliced Napa cabbage
8 ounces firm tofu, cut into
   16 pieces
8 ounces spinach, trimmed,
   washed, and dried

To serve, bring the sauce and platter to the table. Bring to a boil:

8 to 10 cups Brown Beef Stock, 24

Pour the hot stock into a hot pot, fondue pot, or electric skillet at the table and keep at a simmer. With chopsticks or forks, diners hold the meat or vegetables in the simmering stock until done, then dip it into the sauce and eat. When the ingredients on the platter are finished, combine and let stand for 10 minutes:

4 ounces rice stick noodles, broken
   into small pieces
6 cups hot water

Drain and add the noodles to the stock. Ladle the stock and noodles into each bowl over the remaining sauce.

ABOUT
VEGETABLE
SOUPS & STEWS

*I*f you live near a farmers' market and have the time, shop there for the best seasonal produce from your area. As a general seasonal guide, prepare soups and stews using root vegetables and hearty vegetables, such as winter squash, during the cold months; soups and stews using more perishable produce, such as tomatoes and corn, are best cooked during the warm months.

Cut vegetables are often an integral part of a mixed-vegetable soup or stew. Cut them uniformly, to help ensure even cooking. When improvising a soup or stew using cut vegetables, bear in mind that some vegetables take longer than others to cook. Long-cooking vegetables, such as potatoes, should be added first, followed by vegetables such as carrots and green beans, leaving quick-cooking greens, such as spinach and chard, for last. To retain the color in green vegetables, be careful not to cover or overcook the soup. Pureed green-vegetable soups should not cook long, or they will turn gray.

Old-Fashioned Vegetable Soup, 43

Butternut Squash Soup

About 9 cups

Almost any winter squash can be used. For an unusual garnish, rinse and dry the squash seeds, toss them in 1 ½ tea-spoons oil to lightly coat, and bake them along with the squash until browned, then sprinkle them on the soup just before serving.

Preheat the oven to 400°F.
Place cut side down on an oiled baking sheet:

1 medium to large butternut squash (about 3½ pounds), halved and seeded

Bake until the squash can easily be pierced with a fork, about 1 hour. Let cool, then scoop the pulp from the squash skin and discard the skin. Melt or heat in a soup pot, over medium-low heat:

3 tablespoons unsalted butter or vegetable oil

Add and cook, stirring, until tender but not browned, 5 to 10 minutes:

2 large leeks (white part only), cleaned thoroughly and chopped

4 teaspoons minced peeled fresh ginger

Stir in the squash along with:

4 cups *Chicken Stock*, 22, or any vegetable stock, 20

Bring to a simmer and cook, stirring and breaking up the squash with a spoon, for 20 minutes. Puree until smooth. Return to the pot and stir in:

2 cups chicken or vegetable stock

1½ teaspoons salt

Heat through. Ladle into warmed bowls. Garnish with:

Chopped fresh parsley or cilantro
***Croutons*, 124**
Toasted squash seeds (optional)

BUTTERNUT SQUASH

Butternut squash is tan and long necked with a bulb at one end. Inside the squash, the orange flesh is rich, sweet, dry, and superb. These 4- to 6-pound squash have the least waste of any winter squash, since the neck is solid and just the bulb contains seeds.

Cream of Cauliflower Soup

About 6 cups

This recipe is a blueprint for a multitude of vegetable soups, all delicious. To retain the color in green vegetables, such as broccoli, do not cover or overcook the soup.

Heat in a soup pot over medium-low heat until the butter is melted:

¼ cup water or stock
1 tablespoon unsalted butter (optional)

Add and cook, covered, stirring occasionally, until tender but not browned, 5 to 10 minutes:

1 medium onion, coarsely chopped
2 cloves garlic, sliced
⅛ teaspoon ground nutmeg (optional)

Stir in:

4½ cups Chicken Stock, 22, or any vegetable stock, 20

½ cup white wine (optional)
1½ pounds trimmed cauliflower, coarsely chopped

Bring to a boil, reduce the heat, and simmer until the cauliflower is tender, 15 to 20 minutes. Puree until smooth. Return to the pot and stir in:

¼ to ½ cup heavy cream, half-and-half, or milk
½ to 1 teaspoon salt
⅛ teaspoon ground white or black pepper

Simmer briefly and ladle into warmed bowls. Garnish with:

Chopped fresh parsley or snipped fresh dill or chives

Serve with:

Croutons, 124, or crackers

Old-Fashioned Vegetable Soup

About 4 cups

Feel free to vary the vegetables in this soup. For the 3 cups of stock in the recipe, use 2 cups diced vegetables. You could feature the finest vegetables from any one season, changing this soup all the year around. Remember that vegetables cook at varying rates. Start with the heartiest and finish with the most tender.

Bring to a boil over high heat, in a soup pot:

3 cups Classic Beef Stock, 24, Brown Beef Stock, 24, Chicken Stock, 22, or Vegetable Stock, 20
¼ cup diced onions
¼ cup diced carrots
¼ cup sliced celery
¼ cup diced potatoes

¼ cup 1-inch pieces green beans
¼ cup corn kernels
¼ cup baby peas
¼ cup baby lima beans
¼ cup chopped green cabbage (optional)
1 clove garlic, minced
1½ teaspoons tomato paste or ½ cup chopped drained canned or stewed tomatoes

Reduce the heat to low and simmer for 10 minutes. Stir in:

2 tablespoons chopped fresh parsley
Salt and ground black pepper to taste

Ladle into warmed bowls and serve.

CREAM OF ASPARAGUS SOUP

Follow the recipe for *Cream of Cauliflower Soup, left,* omitting the nutmeg and using 4 cups chicken stock and ½ cup dry vermouth or white wine (optional). Trim 1½ pounds asparagus, discarding the tough ends and reserving the tips. Chop the stalks and add to the stock. Simmer for 5 minutes. Puree the soup, adding ¼ to ½ cup heavy cream or half-and-half, salt to taste, ⅛ teaspoon ground black pepper, and the reserved asparagus tips. Simmer for 3 to 5 minutes and serve.

CREAM OF BROCCOLI SOUP

Follow the recipe for *Cream of Caulifower Soup, above left,* substituting broccoli for the cauliflower. Simmer the broccoli until tender but still brightly colored, 5 to 8 minutes. Proceed with the basic recipe, using ground black, not white, pepper.

CREAM OF CARROT SOUP

Follow the recipe for *Cream of Cauliflower Soup, left,* substituting carrots for the cauliflower, 1 tablespoon minced peeled fresh ginger for the garlic, and ½ teaspoon curry powder for the nutmeg; using 4 cups stock and 1 cup fresh orange juice; and omitting the wine. Simmer for 15 minutes. Puree the soup, adding ¼ to ½ cup heavy cream or half-and-half, salt to taste, and ⅛ teaspoon ground black pepper. Simmer briefly and serve.

Mushroom Barley Soup

About 4 cups

Combine and let stand until the mushrooms are softened, about 20 minutes:

¼ ounce dried mushrooms, such as porcini or shiitake (about 3)
1 cup hot water

Remove the mushrooms and squeeze dry with paper towels. Reserve the soaking liquid. Dice the mushrooms finely and reserve. Heat in a soup pot over medium-low heat until the butter is melted:

1 tablespoon unsalted butter
1 tablespoon vegetable oil

Add and cook, stirring, until tender but not browned, 5 to 10 minutes:

5 ounces mushrooms, wiped clean and tough stems removed, coarsely chopped
1 small leek (white part only), cleaned thoroughly and diced
1 small onion, diced
1 medium celery stalk, diced
1 small carrot, diced
2 cloves garlic, minced

Increase the heat slightly and add:

⅓ cup pearl barley

Cook, stirring, until lightly toasted, about 5 minutes. Stir in the reserved diced mushrooms. Strain the soaking liquid through a fine-mesh sieve lined with a dampened paper towel and stir it into the vegetable mixture along with:

4 cups Brown Beef Stock, 24, or Roasted Vegetable Stock, 20

Bring to a boil, reduce the heat, and simmer, partially covered, until the barley is tender, about 40 minutes. Season with:

1 tablespoon snipped fresh dill
½ teaspoon salt
½ teaspoon ground black pepper

Ladle into warmed bowls (opposite) and serve immediately.

Scallion and Mushroom Soup

About 7 cups

This soup uses the whole scallion with stunning results. Select scallions with the crispest leaves with no yellowing or tears, and shiny, bright, stalks. Use your favorite variety of mushroom or a combination of types.

Beat with a wooden spoon until light and fluffy:

4 tablespoons (½ stick) unsalted butter, softened

Add and stir together well:

5 bunches scallions, very finely chopped

Remove to a soup pot and season with:

1 teaspoon salt
½ teaspoon ground white pepper

Cook, covered, over low heat for about 10 minutes. Do not brown the scallions. Remove the pot from the heat. Stir in:

2 tablespoons all-purpose flour

Cook for 1 minute. Whisk in:

4 cups Chicken Stock, 22

Bring to a boil, whisking, over medium heat. Reduce the heat and simmer for 10 minutes. Meanwhile, wipe clean, remove the tough ends of the stems only, and very thinly slice:

12 ounces mushrooms with stems

Remove the soup from the heat and stir in two-thirds of the mushrooms. Immediately push through a sieve or food mill. Stir in:

¼ to ½ cup half-and-half

Gently heat the soup until hot, then stir in the remaining mushrooms. Ladle into warmed bowls. Top each serving with:

Sprinkle of ground red pepper
Dollop of sour cream

PREPARING MUSHROOMS

Clean mushrooms with a soft brush or wipe with a damp cloth. If the mushrooms are truly grimy, rinse them quickly under cold running water and pat dry. Never soak mushrooms—their delicate tissues will absorb water. If desired, slice ⅛ inch off the bottom of the stems to refresh them but do not discard the flavorful stems. If only caps are called for in a recipe, cut the stem flush with the cap. Either chop the stems fairly fine, toss them until lightly browned in a little butter, and add them to the dish or use within a day to flavor something else. Use intense heat when cooking mushrooms, and cook just enough to lightly brown and heat them through.

Minestrone

About 10 cups

Minestrone embraces a legion of hearty vegetable and bean soups from Italy. This one is a melding of styles and is equally good served hot or warm. It uses pancetta, the Italian version of bacon from the pork belly (pancia). Pancetta is not smoked, so it is moister and has a mellower flavor than bacon.

Heat over medium heat in a large soup pot, until the pancetta or bacon has released its fat, 2 to 3 minutes:

2 tablespoons extra-virgin olive oil

1 ounce pancetta or 2 slices bacon, chopped (optional)

Add and cook, stirring, until the greens are beginning to wilt, 5 to 10 minutes:

1 medium onion, chopped

1 large carrot, peeled and chopped

2 medium celery stalks with leaves, minced

One 4-inch sprig fresh rosemary, or 1 teaspoon dried

¼ cup tightly packed fresh basil leaves, chopped

¼ cup tightly packed fresh parsley leaves, chopped

2 cloves garlic, minced

½ small head green cabbage, chopped

3 Swiss chard leaves, washed, dried, and chopped

Cover, and cook until the vegetables are tender, about 10 minutes. Stir in:

One 14-ounce can whole tomatoes, drained and broken into pieces

Cook, stirring, over medium-high heat for 3 to 5 minutes. Stir in:

One 16-ounce can *borlotti* or pinto beans, rinsed and drained, half of them mashed

10 cups *Chicken Stock*, 22, or water

2 teaspoons salt

Bring to a boil, reduce heat, and simmer, partially covered, 30 minutes. Remove the rosemary sprig. Stir in:

4 ounces orzo

Continue to simmer for 15 minutes. Ladle into warmed bowls and drizzle over each serving:

Extra-virgin olive oil

Sprinkle with:

Ground black pepper to taste

Smooth Potato Leek Soup
(Potage Parmentier)

About 8 cups

Potatoes and leeks make magic together. This divine synergy is reflected in two soups. The one here is a simple stock- or water-based soup. Vichyssoise, right, is a smooth, cream-enriched version. Thin the Smooth Potato Leek Soup, *if necessary, with a bit more water or stock. For extra smoothness, push through a sieve after it has been pureed in a food processor.*

Melt in a soup pot, over low heat:

3 tablespoons unsalted butter, or 1 tablespoon butter and ¼ cup water

Add and cook, stirring, until tender but not browned, about 20 minutes:

8 large leeks (white part only), cleaned thoroughly and chopped

Stir in:

3 medium or 2 large baking potatoes, peeled and thinly sliced
5 cups Chicken Stock, 22, *Vegetable Stock*, 20, or water

Bring to a boil, reduce the heat, and simmer until the potatoes are soft, about 30 minutes. Puree until smooth. Season with:

Salt to taste
¼ teaspoon ground white or black pepper

Thin, if necessary, with additional:

Stock or water

Reheat gently, then ladle into warmed bowls.

VICHYSSOISE

The "classic French" soup was invented by French chef Louis Diat around 1910. During the Second World War, when the French spa town of Vichy became the capital of the collaborationist government, this soup was served under a variety of names.

Prepare *Smooth Potato Leek Soup, left,* adding ½ to 1 cup heavy cream, or a combination of milk and cream. Season with salt and ground black pepper to taste and thin if necessary. Garnish with snipped fresh chives, if desired. Serve hot or cold.

PREPARING LEEKS

To julienne or slice leeks, trim off the root and the dark green leaves; if the pale green part is tender, leave about 1 inch attached to the white part. For julienne, cut the leek lengthwise in half, then cut the halves into 2-inch lengths and slice lengthwise. For slices, cut the halves crosswise into half slices.

The layers of a leek can contain dirt, since the white stalks are "blanched," buried in earth to keep them pale, so washing them thoroughly and properly is important. Swish chopped, julienned, or sliced leeks in a large bowl of cool water. Let them stand a few minutes while the dirt falls to the bottom (**1**).

Lift them out with a strainer. Repeat if there is a lot of dirt left in the bowl (**2**).

If you are using leeks that are simply halved lengthwise, soak them in water for 15 minutes to loosen the dirt, gently swish them around, and rinse under cool water, fanning the leaves open as you rinse if they are especially dirty.

Slender leeks are especially nice sliced into salads, grilled and served hot, or steamed and served at room temperature. Thicker leeks are wonderful braised or in soups and stews. Be careful not to overcook leeks, as the layers are very thin.

Cabbage Soup

About 8 cups

We sampled this soup in a Paris bistro, where we discovered that a garnish of Roquefort adds just the right finish. Serve thick slices of baguette that have been toasted alongside—the toasted bread is good for dunking and for soaking up the soup.

Heat in a soup pot over medium-low heat:

2 tablespoons olive or other vegetable oil

Add and cook, stirring, until tender but not browned, 5 to 10 minutes:

2 small leeks (white part only), cleaned thoroughly and chopped

2 medium onions, diced

2 tablespoons chopped garlic

Stir in:

4 cups Chicken Stock, 22

2 cups water

2 large carrots, sliced

¾ teaspoon caraway seeds, or 1 teaspoon if garnishing with Roquefort cheese

Bring to a boil and stir in:

2 small potatoes, peeled and diced

Reduce the heat and simmer until the potatoes are cooked, about 15 minutes. Stir in:

4 cups shredded green cabbage

Continue to simmer until the cabbage is wilted, about 15 minutes, adding a little water to cover, if necessary. Stir in:

1 teaspoon salt

¼ teaspoon ground black pepper, or to taste

¼ cup chopped fresh parsley

Ladle into warmed bowls. Sprinkle each serving with:

1 tablespoon crumbled Roquefort or other blue cheese (optional)

New York Deli Borscht

About 5 cups

About the only thing deli borscht has in common with traditional Russian Borscht, 97, is the presence of beets. This version is light and contains no fat. It is usually served cold but is also satisfying hot. For a more substantial dish, add warm, quartered new potatoes. Though many types of beets are available at market these days, use a red beet for this soup. If you find unwilted greens attached to your beets, wash and dry them, then chop and stir them in at the last minute for an untraditional touch. This borscht can be pureed if a smooth soup is desired.

Combine in a soup pot:

3 cups water

1 pound beets, peeled and cut into thin strips

1 large carrot, peeled and cut into thin strips (optional)

1 clove garlic, minced

Bring to a boil, reduce the heat, and simmer until the beets are tender, 5 to 10 minutes. Stir in:

2 tablespoons fresh lemon juice

1½ teaspoons salt

⅛ teaspoon ground black pepper

Serve hot or cold, garnished with:

Sour cream

Snipped fresh dill

PREPARING BEETS

A source of sugar, beets are an intensely sweet vegetable with a trace of sharpness. Once there was just the crimson beet, but now beets are also gold, orange, white, and candy striped. Beets are best from summer through early winter. When selecting a bunch of beets, choose the bunch with the smallest leaves that are in the best condition. The greens are an indication of freshness for the roots; if they look moist and fresh, the roots will be too.

Cut off the leaves, leaving 1 to 2 inches stem on the beets, and keep the rootlets, or tails, in place (**1**).

Pack the beets and leaves separately in perforated plastic vegetable bags and store in the refrigerator crisper. Scrub beets well before cooking (**2**).

Fresh Tomato Soup

About 4 cups

A simple, clean-tasting soup (opposite).
Heat in a soup pot, over medium-low heat:

2 tablespoons olive oil, preferably extra virgin

Add and cook, stirring, until tender but not browned, 5 to 10 minutes:

1 medium onion, coarsely chopped

Stir in:

3 pounds ripe tomatoes, peeled, seeded, and chopped, with juices

Simmer until the tomatoes are covered in their own liquid, about 25 minutes. Puree until smooth. Return to the pot and stir in:

¾ teaspoon salt
¼ teaspoon ground black pepper

Serve hot or cold.

CREAM OF TOMATO SOUP

Prepare *Fresh Tomato Soup, above.* Stir in ¼ cup heavy cream. Gently heat through. Serve immediately.

PEELING AND SEEDING TOMATOES

Cut a small X in the bottom—do not cut the flesh (**1**). Ease the tomatoes one by one into a pot of boiling water. Leave ripe tomatoes in for about 15 seconds, barely ripe tomatoes in for twice as long. Lift them out with a sieve and drop into a bowl of ice water to stop the cooking. Pull off the skin with the knife (**2**). If the skin sticks, return the tomato to the boiling water for another 10 seconds and repeat. If the dish can use a touch of smoky flavor, hold the tomato on a long-handled fork over the burner, turning it until the skin splits. Do not plunge in water, but peel as above.

Cut it crosswise in half (between the top and bottom). Squeeze each half gently over a strainer set in a bowl to catch the juice, which you can add to soup. Run the tip of a finger into each of the cavities and flick out the mass of seeds (**3**).

Mushroom Soup

About 6 cups

Slice rather than chop the mushrooms for a meaty texture and a handsome look.
Heat in a soup pot over high heat until the butter is melted:

3½ tablespoons extra-virgin olive oil
1 tablespoon unsalted butter or additional olive oil

Add:

1½ pounds mushrooms (preferably at least 12 ounces wild), wiped clean and tough stems removed, sliced

½ cup chopped shallots

Cook, stirring often, until the mushrooms are wilted, about 5 minutes. Add:

3 tablespoons dry sherry or Madeira
5 tablespoons all-purpose flour
1 teaspoon dried thyme, or 1 tablespoon chopped fresh thyme

Reduce the heat to low and cook, stirring constantly and scraping the bottom of the pan, for 5 minutes. Stir in:

4½ cups Brown Chicken Stock, 22, or any vegetable stock, 20
½ to 1 teaspoon salt
¾ teaspoon ground black pepper

Bring to a boil, reduce the heat to medium, and simmer until slightly thickened, about 20 minutes. Ladle into warmed bowls. Garnish with:

Chopped fresh parsley or fresh thyme leaves

Tuscan Bread and Tomato Soup (Pappa al Pomodoro)

About 4 cups

Make this favorite country soup from Tuscany with fresh tomatoes in high summer and eat it at room temperature, or prepare it with canned tomatoes in winter and serve hot. To stay true to the goodness of the soup, use a bread made without sugar.

Preheat the oven to 200°F.

Dry in the oven for 15 to 20 minutes:

2 or 3 thick slices country bread

Alternatively, use stale bread. Heat in a soup pot, over medium heat:

3 tablespoons extra-virgin olive oil

Add and cook, stirring, until beginning to color, about 10 minutes:

1 medium red onion, coarsely chopped

Salt and ground black pepper to taste

Meanwhile, rub the bread on both sides with:

1 clove garlic, halved

Coarsely chop together:

4 large cloves garlic, peeled

⅓ cup tightly packed fresh basil leaves

Reduce the heat to medium-low, stir in the garlic mixture, and cook until the garlic barely colors, 2 to 3 minutes. Add:

1½ pounds ripe tomatoes, peeled, seeded, and coarsely chopped, or one 28-ounce can whole tomatoes, drained and chopped

Pinch of red pepper flakes

Cook, stirring, over medium-high heat until thick and fragrant, about 5 minutes. Stir in:

2 cups *Chicken Stock*, 22, or *Vegetable Stock*, 20

Boil for 2 minutes. Taste and adjust the seasonings. Break up the bread in the bottom of soup bowls. Ladle in the hot soup and top each serving with:

4 fresh basil leaves, torn

Drizzle of extra-virgin olive oil

Parmesan cheese shavings

Serve hot or at room temperature.

Cheddar Cheese Soup

About 6 cups

Serve this soup as a main course.

Melt in a soup pot, over medium heat:

6 tablespoons (¾ stick) unsalted butter

Add and cook until tender, but not browned, 5 to 10 minutes:

1 cup diced onions

1 cup diced celery

¾ cup diced carrots

Sprinkle with:

¼ cup all-purpose flour

Cook, stirring, for 3 to 4 minutes more. Slowly whisk in:

4 cups *Chicken Stock*, 22

Bring the soup to a boil, whisking constantly. Reduce the heat to a simmer and cook until thickened, about 45 minutes. Puree until smooth. Return to the pot, bring to a simmer, and stir in:

1 cup heavy cream or half-and-half

8 ounces Cheddar cheese, grated

1 teaspoon dry mustard

Reduce the heat to low and stir until the cheese is melted. (Do not let the soup boil: if the soup is too hot, the cheese will break down.) Season with:

Hot red pepper sauce to taste (optional)

Worcestershire sauce to taste (optional)

Salt and ground black pepper to taste

If you prefer a thinner soup, thin with additional:

Stock or cream

Garnish with:

***Croutons*, 124**

Finely chopped smoked ham

Chopped cooked broccoli

French Onion Soup

About 8 cups

The secret to this beloved classic is long, slow cooking of the onions to allow their natural sugars to caramelize; this gives the soup its characteristic depth of flavor and rich mahogany color.

Heat in a soup pot over medium-low heat until the butter is melted:

2 tablespoons unsalted butter
2 tablespoons olive oil

Add and stir to coat:

5 medium onions, thinly sliced
Pinch of dried thyme

Cook, stirring occasionally, and keeping a vigilant eye on the onions so they do not scorch, over medium heat. As soon as they start to brown, after about 15 minutes, reduce the heat to medium-low and continue to cook, covered, stirring more often, until the onions are a rich brown color, about 40 minutes. Stir in:

2 tablespoons dry sherry or cognac

Increase the heat to high and cook, stirring constantly, until all the sherry has cooked off. Stir in:

3½ cups Brown Beef Stock, 24, *Roasted Vegetable Stock*, 20, or *Brown Chicken Stock*, 22

Bring to a boil, reduce the heat, and simmer, partially covered, for 20 minutes.

Season with:

1 to 1½ teaspoons salt
¼ to ½ teaspoon ground black pepper

Place 8 ovenproof soup bowls or crocks on a baking sheet. Ladle the hot soup into the bowls and top each serving with:

1 to 3 slices French bread, toasted if fresh

Sprinkle each bowl with:

3 tablespoons grated Gruyère cheese

Broil or bake in a 450°F oven until the cheese is melted and starting to brown. Serve immediately.

Gazpacho

About 6 cups

There are numerous varieties of gazpacho in Spain—a white one from Málaga, made with garlic, bread, and almonds and garnished with green grapes; a cumin-scented one from Granada; even a stewlike game-filled version (called gaspatxos*) from Alicante. The familiar version is this one—an Andalusian "pureed salad" of summery vegetables (opposite). Classic gazpachos are thickened with bread, although many contemporary recipes, like this one, omit it. We have added a nontraditional jalapeño pepper for more bite. Gazpacho is better served the day it is made, but if preparing it for the next day, use half the jalapeño, as the heat increases with time.*

Finely chop, but do not puree, in a food processor or blender:

1 medium cucumber, peeled, seeded, and coarsely chopped

1 medium green bell pepper, coarsely chopped

Remove to a large bowl. Finely chop in the processor:

1 small onion, coarsely chopped
⅓ cup packed fresh parsley leaves

Remove to the bowl. Add to the processor and finely chop:

2½ pounds ripe tomatoes, peeled, seeded, and coarsely chopped

Remove to the bowl. Add:

1 cup tomato juice
¼ cup red wine vinegar
3 tablespoons extra-virgin olive oil
2 cloves garlic, minced
1 fresh jalapeño pepper, seeded and minced, or a dash of hot red pepper sauce (optional)
2 teaspoons salt

Stir well. Refrigerate for at least 2 hours. Serve in chilled bowls.

CUCUMBERS

These quenching vegetables—about 96 percent water—are cucurbitas, part of a huge family that includes squashes. They may be field or hot-house grown, long and slender or stubby or round, and nearly seedless or filled with seeds. We eat them when they are green and immature. The round lemon cucumber, however, we eat when mature and pale yellow. Cucumbers' season is summer and early autumn, although they are nearly always in the market. Select cucumbers that are a rich green and sound and firm—no soft spots, bruises, or cuts. Usually the smallest cucumbers are the least mature and therefore have the smallest seeds. Store in perforated plastic bags in the refrigerator.

Grilled Tomato Soup

About 4 cups

An intensely flavored soup that is delicious hot or cold. The grilling brings out the sweetness of the tomato and adds smoky flavor. If you cannot grill the tomatoes, broil them as close as you can to the heating element. The soup may thicken more when it is cold than when it is hot. To thin, add a little more stock or a bit of water.

Preheat the grill or broiler.
Halve through the circumference and seed:

3 pounds ripe tomatoes

Brush both sides with:

Olive oil, preferably extra virgin

If grilling, simply place on the grill. If broiling, arrange skin side up in a roasting pan. Grill or broil the tomatoes on both sides until golden and slightly charred. Remove to a platter or leave in the roasting pan. Heat in a soup pot, over medium-low heat:

2 tablespoons olive oil, preferably extra virgin

Add and cook, stirring often, until tender but not brown, 5 to 10 minutes:

1 medium onion, coarsely chopped

Add the tomatoes and stir, breaking up the tomatoes with the spoon. Stir in:

1 cup *Chicken Stock*, 22
1 tablespoon dry white wine
1 clove garlic, minced

Simmer until the tomatoes are softened and have released their juices, 25 to 30 minutes. Puree until smooth. Strain, if you wish, to remove the skin. Stir in:

¾ teaspoon salt
¼ teaspoon ground black pepper

Let cool to room temperature and refrigerate until cold. Just before serving, stir in:

2 tablespoons fresh lemon juice
1 teaspoon balsamic vinegar
2 tablespoons chopped fresh basil

Adjust the seasonings, ladle into bowls, and garnish each with:

1 sprig fresh basil
1 thin slice lemon, seeded (optional)

Tomato Jalapeño Chilaquiles

About 4 cups

Heat a medium, heavy skillet or griddle (preferably cast iron) over medium heat until hot. Place in the skillet:

1 to 2 fresh jalapeño peppers
2 large cloves garlic, unpeeled

Roast, turning occasionally, until the chili peppers are blistered and blackened on all sides and the garlic is soft to the touch, 10 to 15 minutes. When cool enough to handle, peel the garlic. Place in a food processor or blender with the chili peppers. Coarsely chop using on-off pulses. Add:

One 28-ounce can whole tomatoes, drained

Process until the mixture is coarsely pureed. Heat in a soup pot over medium heat:

1½ teaspoons vegetable oil

Add and cook until nicely browned, about 8 to 10 minutes:

½ small onion, thinly sliced

Increase the heat to medium-high and add the tomato mixture. Cook, stirring, until the mixture is darkened and slightly thickened, about 5 minutes. Reduce the heat to medium-low and stir in:

3 cups *Chicken Stock*, 22, *Chicken Broth*, 29, *Vegetable Stock*, 20, or *Vegetable Broth*, 29

Simmer, stirring occasionally, for 15 minutes. Season with:

½ to 1 teaspoon salt (depending on the saltiness of the broth)

Just before serving, bring the mixture to a boil and add:

8 ounces thick homemade-style tortilla chips

Stir to coat the chips well, then increase the heat to medium-high and boil rapidly, stirring gently and often, until the chips are softened (but are still a little chewy) and the sauce is reduced to a medium-thick consistency, 2 to 3 minutes for thinner chips, 4 to 5 minutes for thicker chips. Immediately spoon the *chilaquiles* onto a warm deep platter. Serve garnished with:

¼ cup finely crumbled queso fresco or grated Monterey Jack cheese
2 tablespoons chopped fresh cilantro (optional)
2 tablespoons sour cream thinned with a little milk (optional)

Okra Stew

4 to 6 servings

In this recipe, okra is kept whole to reduce its thickening effect. Soaking okra in vinegar helps reduce its sticky juices even further. Do not cook this stew in an aluminum, iron, or unlined copper pot—these metals react with okra. This stew is delicious served over grits.

Combine in a bowl and marinate for 30 minutes:

1 pound fresh or thawed frozen whole okra, stems trimmed
½ cup red wine vinegar
2 tablespoons salt

Drain and rinse under cold running water. Heat in a large skillet over medium heat:

3 tablespoons olive or vegetable oil

Add:

2 onions, chopped
2 cloves garlic, minced

Cook until lightly colored around the edges, 4 to 5 minutes. Add:

1 pound fresh or canned tomatoes, peeled, seeded, and diced
1 teaspoon sugar

Cook over medium-low heat until thick, about 30 minutes. Add the okra and season with:

Salt and ground black pepper to taste

Cook until the okra is tender, about 10 minutes more. Serve in bowls.

OKRA

Okra pods are the young seedpods of a beautiful plant related to hollyhocks and hibiscus. Whole pods, untouched by a knife, are steamed or sautéed for just 3 to 5 minutes. The pods emerge tender but still crisp. The pods are not gummy. When desired, the pods can be cut into thick slices so they can release their sweet mucilaginous ingredient for a natural thickening. The secret to superb eating is to choose pods no longer than your little finger. Pods should be heavy for their size, moist and plump, blemish free, with stems intact.

Cold Avocado Soup

About 4 cups

Flavorful ripe Haas avocados, the kind with the bumpy skins, are best for this colorful summer soup.

Puree in a food processor or food mill until smooth:

**2 ripe Haas avocados (about
   1 pound), peeled and pitted**

1 small clove garlic, chopped

Stir in:

2 cups buttermilk

4 teaspoons fresh lime juice

¼ teaspoon salt

Pinch of ground red pepper

Remove to a bowl and refrigerate until cold. Thin, if necessary, with:

¼ to ½ cup buttermilk or water

Taste and adjust the seasonings. Ladle the soup into chilled bowls and garnish with:

1½ cups *Salsa Fresca*, 118

**2 tablespoons sour cream or yogurt
   (optional)**

**½ pound fresh lump crabmeat,
   picked over, or cooked shrimp
   (optional)**

AVOCADOS

Grown in southern California and Florida, avocados are available year-round. California specializes in the Haas, a purplish black, pebbly skinned avocado of the Guatemalan type. Haas avocados weigh about 8 ounces and have superior flavor. Their flesh is so rich and buttery because it contains twice as much fat as the smaller, smooth-skinned, green Mexican type of avocados that are grown in Florida. (California's other avocado, smooth green Fuerte, is probably a Guatemalan-Mexican hybrid.) Although fat means calories, most fat in avocados is monounsaturated, the friendly sort found in olives. From southern Florida and Hawaii also comes the yellow-skinned West Indian avocado. Should you find 1- to 2-ounce cocktail avocados (they are Fuertes or Mexican fruits with no seed, remnants of dropped pollinated flowers), prepare as usual.

Choose an unblemished fruit that is heavy for its size, ideally one that is tender when gently pressed between your hands. Ripe avocados are rare at the market, so plan to buy them about 3 days before you will need them. Until it is cut, a stone-hard avocado will ripen in a brown paper bag kept at room temperature out of the sun in about that much time. Slightly overripe fruit can be used for mashing but not slicing. Refrigerate ripe fruits for up to 2 days. Avocado flesh quickly darkens when exposed to air. This does not affect quality or flavor but mars the beauty of the fruit. To prevent avocados from darkening, immediately rub cut surfaces with a slice of citrus—the more the better. Avocados turn bitter when cooked, so enjoy them raw. When adding avocado to cooked dishes, do it at the last minute, off the heat.

Provençal Vegetable Soup (Soupe au Pistou)

About 10 cups

This signature dish of the south of France is a light and flavorful vegetable soup (opposite).

Heat in a large soup pot, over medium-low heat:

2 tablespoons olive oil, preferably extra virgin

Add and cook, stirring, until tender but not browned, 5 to 10 minutes:

1 medium onion, chopped

1 small leek (white and tender green parts), cleaned thoroughly and chopped

1 medium carrot, peeled and chopped

1 large celery stalk, chopped

Stir in:

2 medium, ripe tomatoes, peeled, seeded, and chopped

1 small potato, peeled and chopped

8 cups water

2 teaspoons salt

Pinch of saffron threads (optional)

Bring to a boil, reduce the heat, and simmer until the potatoes are tender, about 30 minutes. Stir in:

One 15½- or 19-ounce can cannellini or great Northern beans, rinsed and drained, or 1 to 2 cups cooked (⅓ to ⅔ cup dried), 67

Small handful of thin spaghetti, broken up, or short macaroni

1 small zucchini, quartered lengthwise and sliced

4 ounces green beans, cut into 1-inch pieces

Simmer just until the pasta is tender. Meanwhile, make the pistou. Puree in a blender, until smooth:

2 cups fresh basil leaves

2 cloves garlic, chopped

¼ cup extra-virgin olive oil

Remove the soup from the heat. Immediately stir in the pistou along with:

⅔ cup coarsely grated Parmesan cheese

1 teaspoon ground black pepper

Ladle into warmed bowls to serve hot, or serve at room temperature or cold.

Roasted Red Pepper Soup

About 8 cups

This is a rustic-style soup that is full of texture and sweet red pepper flavor. If fresh fennel is not available, use an equal amount of chopped celery and increase the fennel seeds to 1¼ teaspoons. Serve either hot or cold with grilled garlic toasts.

Preheat the broiler.

Arrange skin side up in a roasting pan:

6 large red bell peppers, quartered and seeded

Trim if necessary so the peppers lay flat and brush them lightly with:

Olive oil

Place under the broiler and cook until the skins are thoroughly blistered and blackened. Remove the pan to a rack. When cool enough to handle, peel the peppers, discarding the skins, and cut into long strips. Heat in a soup pot over medium-low heat:

3 tablespoons olive oil

Add and cook, stirring, until tender but not browned, 10 to 15 minutes:

2 cups chopped onions

1 cup diced carrots

1 cup chopped fennel bulb

Stir in:

5 cups *Chicken Stock*, 22, or *Vegetable Stock*, 20

1 cup dry white wine

3 tablespoons medium-grain rice, preferably Arborio

2 tablespoons chopped fresh basil, or 2 teaspoons dried

1 tablespoon chopped fresh rosemary, or 1 teaspoon dried

1 teaspoon fennel seeds

⅛ teaspoon red pepper flakes

Bring to a boil, reduce the heat, and simmer partially covered, until the peppers and rice are very tender, about 30 minutes. Meanwhile, make the garlic toasts. Preheat the grill or broiler.

Arrange on a baking sheet:

8 slices Italian bread or 16 slices French bread

Lightly brush the slices on both sides with:

Olive oil, preferably extra virgin

Rub on both sides with:

1 to 2 cloves garlic, halved

Grill or broil the bread on both sides until golden. When the soup is done, puree until smooth. Return the soup to the pot and season with:

Salt and ground black pepper to taste

2 to 3 drops balsamic vinegar

Ladle into bowls or let cool to room temperature and refrigerate. Serve with the garlic toasts. If serving chilled, taste cold and adjust the seasonings.

Portuguese Greens Soup (Caldo Verde)

About 10 cups

This hearty soup is from the province of Minho, Portugal, which is famous for its cooking. Caldo verde was brought to us by the Portuguese communities in Cape Cod, Rhode Island, and other parts of the eastern seaboard.

Heat in a large soup pot, over medium-low heat:

1½ tablespoons olive or other vegetable oil

Add and cook, stirring, until tender but not browned, 5 to 10 minutes:

1 medium onion, chopped

2 cloves garlic, minced

Stir in:

8 cups water, or 6 cups water and 2 cups Chicken Stock, 22

4 medium potatoes, peeled and thinly sliced

1½ teaspoons salt

½ teaspoon ground black pepper

Bring to a boil, reduce the heat, and simmer until the potatoes are soft,

about 20 minutes. Remove the pot from the heat. Using a potato masher, lightly mash the potatoes right in the pot. (This will give the soup a chunky texture.) Heat in a medium skillet, over medium-high heat:

½ teaspoon vegetable oil (optional)

Add and cook, stirring, until browned:

6 ounces Portuguese linguiça or chorizo sausage, thinly sliced

Add to the soup pot. Pour 1 cup of the soup into the skillet. Scrape up the browned bits and return the liquid and browned bits to the soup. Simmer for 5 minutes. Stir in:

4 cups shredded kale, Swiss chard, or collard leaves (from a 6- to 8-ounce bunch), washed and dried

Simmer for 5 minutes. Stir in:

2 tablespoons fresh lemon juice

Ladle into warmed bowls.

KALE, SWISS CHARD, AND COLLARD GREENS

Kale (left) deserves to be appreciated as much as spinach. Most culinary kales have blue, magenta, or grayish leaves that are curled, crinkly, or deeply cut. Their leaves have a delicate cabbage taste and are sweetest when grown in cold climates and picked after a frost.

When you see the large, ruffled, rich green leaves of Swiss chard at the market, you might imagine they have a flamboyant flavor to match. In fact, chard has a more delicate taste than spinach, and very young chard leaves are as mild as lettuce. The Swiss is a puzzlement; there is nothing Swiss about this close relative of beets. Chard leaves may be green with white ribs or burgundy with crimson ribs. (Burgundy-colored chard is also known as rhubarb chard.) But there is more to this vegetable than leaves. The fleshy ribs can be prepared separately; they taste like earthy celery.

Collard's large, smooth, dark green leaves have a flavor somewhere between cabbage or kale and turnip greens, fellow members of the mustard family. Depending on their size and age, they can be mild and sweet or mustardy. Collards do not form a head but grow on stalks that are too tough to eat. The leaves cook fairly quickly.

Select bunches of kale, Swiss chard, and collard greens with the crispest, brightest leaves and no yellowing, tears, or holes. Store in perforated plastic vegetable bags in the refrigerator crisper.

Southeast Asian Curried Vegetable Stew

6 servings

Heat in a wok or large saucepan over medium heat:

1 tablespoon vegetable oil

Add:

1½ teaspoons cumin seeds

Cook, stirring, for 1 to 2 minutes. Process in a food processor to a smooth paste:

½ medium onion, coarsely chopped

One 1-inch piece fresh ginger, peeled and quartered

4 cloves garlic, peeled

1 to 2 medium fresh jalapeño peppers, seeded

1 teaspoon ground turmeric

2 tablespoons water

Add the paste to the cumin seeds and cook, stirring often, over medium-low heat for 3 to 5 minutes. Stir in:

One 14-ounce can unsweetened coconut milk

½ cup chicken or vegetable stock

1 pound sweet potatoes, peeled and cut into ¾-inch cubes

Bring to a boil. Reduce the heat and simmer, covered, for 8 minutes. Stir in:

3 cups broccoli florets and cut stems

One 10½-ounce package firm tofu, or 8 ounces tempeh, cut into ¾-inch cubes

Simmer, covered, until the broccoli is tender, about 10 minutes. Add and bring to a boil:

1 large tomato, coarsely chopped

Combine and stir in:

3 tablespoons fresh lime juice

2 tablespoons water

2 tablespoons all-purpose flour

Boil, stirring, until thickened, about 1 minute. Stir in:

½ to 1 teaspoon chili paste

Salt and ground black pepper to taste

Arrange on a serving platter:

6 cups hot cooked brown or white rice

Spoon the vegetable curry over the rice and sprinkle generously with:

Finely chopped fresh cilantro

Chopped cashews (optional)

Root Vegetable and Seitan Stew

8 servings

Vary the vegetables for the stew depending upon availability and preference. Turnips, rutabagas, sweet potatoes, kohlrabi, and fennel are other delicious choices.

Heat in a large Dutch oven or heavy pot over low heat:

2 tablespoons vegetable oil

Add:

1 cup sliced onions
1 cup sliced leeks (white part only)
1 cup sliced peeled carrots
5 cloves garlic, minced

Cook, covered, stirring occasionally, until very soft, about 20 minutes. Stir in:

1 tablespoon sugar

Cook, uncovered, stirring occasionally, over medium to medium-low heat until the onions are caramelized, 10 to 15 minutes. Stir in:

4 cups chopped mixed mushrooms, such as portobello, shiitake, and/or oyster mushrooms

Cook for 3 to 4 minutes, then stir in:

3 tablespoons all-purpose flour

Cook for 1 minute. Cut into ¾- to 1-inch cubes and add:

1 medium baking potato
1 medium parsnip, peeled
1 small butternut squash, peeled and seeded

Stir in:

2½ cups *Vegetable Stock,* 20
½ cup dry white wine or vegetable stock
½ teaspoon dried rosemary
½ teaspoon dried thyme
2 or 3 pinches of freshly grated or ground nutmeg

Bring to a boil. Reduce the heat and simmer, covered, for 20 minutes. Stir in:

1½ cups halved small Brussels sprouts
1½ cups chopped plum tomatoes
1½ cups chopped unpeeled Jerusalem artichokes
1 pound seitan, cut into 1-inch cubes

Simmer, covered, for 20 minutes more. Season with:

Salt and ground black pepper to taste

If desired, serve over:

Hot cooked bulgur or brown rice

SEITAN

Also called wheat gluten or wheat meat, seitan is a protein-rich Asian meat substitute, but one that uses wheat instead of soy (as tofu does). It was invented by Buddhist monks centuries ago to bring the texture and protein of meat to their vegetarian diet. Seitan is made by kneading and washing a dough of very high protein flour to develop the wheat's gluten and remove its starch and bran. Shaped into chunks, balls, cutlets, or a large sausage, the grayish gluten is then simmered gently in stock for several hours. It swells, absorbs flavor, and becomes firm with cooking.

You can shortcut the iffy process of making seitan at home by starting with a packaged mix or buying ready-to-use seitan in jars or refrigerated tubs or packages. Check the expiration date on refrigerated seitan; refrigerate for no longer than a week after opening or freeze it for 3 to 4 weeks. Ready-made seitan is sold in the stock it was cooked in, which may be flavored with soy sauce and ginger or with Mexican, Italian, Thai, or other seasonings.

Seitan can be prepared in any way that will disguise its grayness but should not be cooked much longer than necessary to heat and sauce it thoroughly, as lengthy cooking brings out a bitter taste. It is a nice addition to quick-cooking stews.

Seitan provides 16 grams protein per 4-ounce serving, has no fat, and is rich in iron. Keep in mind that seitan should be avoided by anyone sensitive to gluten, especially those with celiac disease.

ABOUT **LEGUME** SOUPS & STEWS

*F*or the contemporary cook, legume soups and stews have many advantages, besides their great nutrition: they are easy to prepare in large batches, they freeze well, the raw materials are easily kept on hand, and they require little attention while cooking.

Pureed bean soups can be passed through a sieve or food mill to eliminate the skins. If a legume soup or stew becomes too thick during long simmering, simply thin it with a bit of water or stock. Do not puree for a chunkier soup.

Cuban Black Bean Soup (Sopa de Frijol Negro), 70

Soaking Beans

Whether or not to soak beans before cooking is a hot topic today. Many noted food professionals, whose opinions we hold in high regard, argue that fresh dried beans do not benefit from presoaking before cooking. Heating the legumes to boiling and then simmering them until they swell with water and soften can be done in one continuous process. In order to ensure success with this method, the beans must be of high quality and fresh. Given the limited availability of high-quality fresh dried beans, presoaking the beans first is kinder, both to the bean and to the cook. Not only does it save anywhere from 30 minutes to over an hour on the stove, but it also treats the seed coat more gently than steady simmering, so that the shape of the bean holds without breaking. At high elevations, where simmering times will be extended by the lower temperature of the boiling water, soaking for up to 24 hours is good time-saving insurance.

Before you prepare any legumes, spread them in a pan or large colander and remove any tiny stones that may have accompanied them out of the field. Then rinse the beans very well under cold water, raking them with your fingers to get rid of any clumps of dirt.

Our preferred soaking method is to heat the soaking water, which hastens the swelling of the beans. For a gentle quick-soak, pour boiling water over the beans to cover by 2 inches, cover, let stand until the beans have swelled to at least twice their size and have absorbed most of the water, and then drain, discarding the soaking liquid. This will take at least an hour and possibly longer, but the beans will remain firm and keep their shape when cooked.

Another way to soak beans is to place them in a large bowl or pot and add water to cover by at least 2 inches. Cover and let stand for up to 24 hours; refrigerate to prevent fermentation if the kitchen is very warm. The beans will swell to triple their dried size. Drain well and discard the soaking liquid.

A third method, which risks breaking some bean skins, is to place the beans in a saucepan, add water to cover by 2 inches, and heat to boiling; then reduce the heat and simmer for 2 minutes. Let stand, covered, for 1 hour. Or microwave 1 pound beans and 4 cups water in a covered 3- to 4-quart casserole on high to boiling, 12 to 17 minutes, and then on medium for 2 minutes. Stir and let stand, covered, for 1 hour. With all three soaking methods, be sure to rinse and drain the beans before the final cooking.

Cooking Beans

To cook beans, place them in a large pot and add cold water to cover by 2 inches. Bring to a boil over high heat; skim off the foam that rises to the surface. Reduce the heat to low and cover; simmer, stirring and skimming occasionally, until the beans are tender. Do not boil rapidly or the abrasion will loosen the bean skins. If the pot threatens to boil over, partially remove the cover. Cook beans uncovered if you have seasoned the liquid and want some of it to evaporate to concentrate the flavor or to thicken the dish. Baking is an alternative to boiling, especially with black, red, and white beans; the benefits are better shape and creamier texture.

Beans readily absorb seasonings from water. A classic way to add flavor is to bury one or two smoked ham hocks or a ham bone in the beans; smoked turkey can be substituted. Add a couple of bay leaves and an onion studded with a half-dozen cloves to the ham or turkey, and the beans will taste smoky and slightly spicy. Simmer beans with chopped onions and carrots to sweeten them; use at least a cup of each with a pound of beans, because the water will dilute their impact. Whole allspice and a piece of cinnamon stick are especially good with black or red beans; wrap spices in cheesecloth or place in a tea ball for easy removal. Whole bay leaves and dried thyme or rosemary bring nice herbal notes to white and lima beans. The possibilities are infinite and come with only a few caveats. First, expect that any salty ingredients, such as smoked meats, will slow the cooking a little; do not add plain salt until near the end, when the beans have already softened. Do not add tomatoes, citrus, vinegar, molasses, or any other acidic ingredients until near the end, after the beans are tender; acid, like salt, prevents the beans from softening. This principle is conveniently applied in reverse when you make Boston baked beans: the precooked beans do not turn mushy when baked for hours because the added molasses and tomatoes keep the skins firm.

If you want relatively firm beans to use in recipes that call for further cooking without acidic ingredients, remove a few beans and pinch them for tenderness at the low end of the cooking time range. If you want very soft beans for a soup or stew, you may decide to cook them longer than suggested. If so, be sure there is enough water in the pot to keep the beans from drying out. Add more as needed, for the beans will not continue to soften without more water to absorb.

Canned beans can be substituted cup for cup in recipes that call for cooked beans, but they are almost always softer and less flavorful. Since brands vary in quality, it is worth trying different ones. Rinsing canned beans improves the taste a little and removes excess salt. To rinse well, put the beans in a large sieve set in a pot or bowl and let cold water run over the beans until the pot is filled, raking the beans with your fingers, and drain, repeat, and then drain well. For a full 2 cups cooked beans, you will need a large can, 19 or 20 ounces. The smaller 15- or 16-ounce can holds only 1½ to 1¾ cups.

Lentil Soup

About 10 cups

Heat in a large soup pot, over medium-low heat:

3 tablespoons olive oil

Add and cook, stirring, until tender but not browned, 5 to 10 minutes:

3 medium carrots, peeled and diced

3 medium celery stalks, diced

1 large onion, diced

3 cloves garlic, minced

2 ounces prosciutto or pancetta, or 4 slices bacon, diced (optional)

Stir in:

8 cups water

2 cups lentils, picked over and rinsed

One 14½-ounce can diced tomatoes, drained

1 teaspoon dried thyme

Bring to a boil, reduce the heat, and simmer until the lentils are tender, 30 to 45 minutes. Stir in:

1½ teaspoons balsamic vinegar

2 teaspoons salt (1 teaspoon if using the meat)

1 teaspoon ground black pepper

Ladle into warmed bowls.

Split Pea Soup

About 6 cups

Try this soup on a cold winter day, seasoned with plenty of freshly ground black pepper.

Combine in a soup pot:

8 cups cold water

1 small ham hock

1 pound split green peas (about 2 cups)

Bring to a boil, reduce the heat, and simmer for 1 hour.

Stir in:

1 large carrot, peeled and diced

1 large celery stalk, diced

1 medium onion, diced

2 cloves garlic, minced

1 *Bouquet Garni*, 17

Simmer until the ham hock and peas are tender, about 1 hour more.

Season with:

Salt and lots of ground black pepper to taste

Remove the ham hock. Discard the bone, skin, and fat; dice the meat. Return it to the soup. For a thicker soup, simmer to the desired consistency. Stir to blend before serving. Ladle into warmed bowls.

Garnish with:

Croutons, 124

SPLIT PEAS

Green split peas remind us how good peas taste, with a flavor more intense than that of young green peas and a much denser texture. Yellow split peas are similar but blander, providing a more neutral backdrop for all kinds of seasonings. Both green and yellow split peas cook to a thick, creamy texture that is perfect for soups such as classic split pea. The technique of steaming dried peas to loosen their skins, then peeling and splitting them to hasten cooking, has been practiced in India for thousands of years. The resulting products, shiny green and yellow split peas, are so convenient to use that they have largely displaced dried whole peas, with their gray-green skins, on supermarket shelves. There are other advantages to using split peas. Whole dried peas need soaking; split peas do not. Because they have no skins, split peas lose their shape in the pot; for the same reason, they can be cooked with salt, for there are no skins to toughen.

Caribbean Red Bean Stew with Pork

4 to 6 servings

This stew makes a hearty meal.
Pick over, rinse, and soak, 66:

**1½ cups dried red kidney, pinto,
  or small red beans**

Drain. Combine the beans in a large saucepan with:

8 cups water
1 small onion
1 leafy celery top
1 bay leaf
1 clove garlic, peeled
One 3-inch cinnamon stick

Bring to a boil. Reduce the heat and simmer, covered, until the beans are tender, about 1 hour. Drain, reserving 4 cups of the cooking liquid. Discard the vegetables and seasonings. Heat in a large saucepan over medium heat:

1 tablespoon olive oil

Add and brown on all sides:

**1 pound trimmed boneless pork,
  cut into 1-inch cubes**

Add:

**1 large onion, cut into ½-inch
  cubes**
**1 green bell pepper, cut into
  1-inch pieces**

**2 cups 1-inch cubes peeled sweet
  potato**
**1 tablespoon coarsely chopped
  garlic**
1 teaspoon salt

Cook, stirring, until the onions are golden, 12 to 15 minutes. Add:

2 teaspoons hot paprika

Stir to blend. Add the cooked beans and the reserved cooking liquid. Bring to a boil. Reduce the heat and simmer, uncovered, until the pork is tender and the stew is thick, about 1 hour. Serve hot.

U.S. Senate Bean Soup

About 6 cups

This soup has been on the U.S. Senate restaurant menu since 1901.

Pick over, rinse, and soak, 66:

1¼ cups small dried white beans, such as pea or navy

Drain and place in a soup pot along with:

7 cups cold water

1 small ham hock

Bring to a boil, reduce the heat, and simmer until the beans are tender, about 1¼ hours. Remove the ham hock. Discard the bone, skin, and fat; dice the meat. Return it to the pot along with:

1 large onion, diced

3 medium celery stalks with leaves, chopped

1 large potato, peeled and finely diced

2 cloves garlic, minced

1½ teaspoons salt

½ teaspoon ground black pepper

Simmer until the potatoes are quite soft, 20 to 30 minutes. Remove from the heat and mash with a potato masher until the soup is a bit creamy. Stir in:

2 tablespoons chopped fresh parsley

Ladle into warmed bowls.

Cuban Black Bean Soup (Sopa de Frijol Negro)

About 8 cups

Pick over, rinse, and soak, 66:

1 pound dried black beans (about 2½ cups)

Heat in a large soup pot over medium-low heat:

2 tablespoons vegetable oil

Add and cook, stirring, until tender but not browned, 5 to 10 minutes:

2 medium onions, chopped

3 medium celery stalks, diced

4 cloves garlic, minced

½ Scotch bonnet pepper or 2 to 3 fresh jalapeño peppers, seeded and diced

Drain and add the black beans along with:

11 cups water

1 large ham hock (optional)

Bring to a boil, reduce the heat, and simmer until the beans are tender, about 2 hours. Remove the ham hock if using. Discard the bone, skin, and fat; dice the meat. Puree the beans in a food processor or by passing them through a food mill. Return to the pot. Stir in the meat along with:

¼ to ½ cup dry sherry or rum

2 teaspoons salt (less if using the ham hock)

Simmer for several minutes to heat through. Thin with additional water if necessary. Stir in:

2 tablespoons fresh lemon juice (optional)

Garnish at the table with any or all of the following:

Lemon wedges

Chopped onions

Steamed white rice

Chopped hard-boiled eggs

Chopped scallions

Wild Caribbean Black Bean Chili

8 to 10 servings

To the traditional chili seasonings of cumin and chili powder, this Caribbean-inspired black bean version adds the tang of citrus and the blistering floral heat of the habanero pepper. Jalapeño peppers, which can be substituted, vary considerably in their heat from totally mild to quite hot varieties found in farmers' markets.

Pick over and rinse:

4 cups dried black beans

Drain. Combine the beans in a large pot with water to cover by 2 inches. Bring to a boil. Reduce the heat to low and simmer, partially covered, until almost tender, about 1 hour. Drain. Heat in the same large pot over medium heat until hot but not smoking:

¼ cup vegetable oil

Add:

4 medium onions, finely diced

Cook, stirring occasionally, until just starting to brown, 8 to 10 minutes. Add:

¼ cup minced garlic

1 to 2 tablespoons minced habanero peppers or 6 to 8 tablespoons minced fresh jalapeño peppers

Cook, stirring, for 1 minute. Add, stir together well, and bring to a simmer:

¼ cup chili powder

¼ cup ground cumin

2 tablespoons sugar

2 teaspoons salt

2 teaspoons ground black pepper

3 teaspoons grated orange zest

1½ cups fresh orange juice

2 teaspoons grated lime zest

¾ cup fresh lime juice

One 28-ounce can crushed tomatoes

6 cups water

Stir in the reserved black beans. Return to a simmer, cover, and reduce the heat to low. Cook, partially covered, checking occasionally and adding more water as needed, until the beans are just soft to the bite, 1½ to 2 hours. Adjust the seasonings and serve, garnished, if desired, with:

Sour cream

Chopped fresh cilantro

Minced scallions

Lime wedges for squeezing

HABANERO PEPPER

The habanero pepper is reputed to be the hottest pepper of all chilies. These lantern-shaped peppers pack tremendous fruity and floral flavors and aromas, along with an incredible punch. Usually found in markets colored green, yellow-orange, or bright orange, habaneros are sometimes mislabeled as the equally hot but less floral Scotch bonnet. Used extensively in the Yucatán, they have become increasingly popular in this country in salsas, sauces, and condiments. They measure about 1½ inches long and 1½ inches wide at the stem end.

Mediterranean White Bean Soup

About 6 cups

Simple and aromatic, this is what used to be called a "pantry soup," because it uses household staples. Feel free to add a touch of extra chopped fresh herbs such as thyme, fennel leaves, or sage.

Pick over, rinse, and soak, 66:

1 cup large dried white beans, such as cannellini or great Northern

Drain and place in a soup pot along with:

7 cups water

¾ teaspoon dried rosemary

8 cloves garlic, chopped or sliced

Bring to a boil, reduce the heat, and simmer until the beans are tender, 1 to 1½ hours. Stir in:

½ cup chopped ripe tomatoes

¼ cup chopped fresh parsley

¼ cup extra-virgin olive oil

4 teaspoons red wine vinegar

2 teaspoons salt

½ teaspoon ground black pepper

Ladle into warmed bowls.

Georgia Peanut Soup

About 4 cups

Peanuts are among the many culinary treasures brought to the United States by slaves from Africa. If you are preparing this dish a day or so ahead, use less ground red pepper and hot red pepper sauce, as the heat intensifies over time.

Heat in a soup pot, over medium-low heat until the butter is melted:

2 tablespoons unsalted butter
1 tablespoon vegetable oil

Add and cook, stirring, until tender but not browned, about 5 to 10 minutes:

1 small onion, chopped
2 medium celery stalks, chopped

Stir in:

2 tablespoons all-purpose flour

Reduce the heat to low and cook, stirring, for 5 minutes. Stir in:

4 cups Chicken Stock, 22, or Brown Chicken Stock, 22

Simmer, stirring often, until the soup begins to thicken, about 5 minutes. Stir in:

1 cup unsalted smooth peanut butter
¼ cup heavy cream or half-and-half

1½ teaspoons salt
1 teaspoon ground red pepper
1 teaspoon hot red pepper sauce

Heat through but do not boil. Stir in:

2 teaspoons fresh lemon juice

Ladle into warmed bowls. Garnish with:

3 tablespoons chopped dry-roasted peanuts
¼ cup chopped scallion greens

Sweet Potato and Peanut Stew

6 servings

Omit the ground beef or turkey for a vegetarian version.

Heat in a large, heavy saucepan over medium-low heat:

¼ cup peanut oil

Add:

1 onion, chopped
1 red or green bell pepper, chopped
1 fresh jalapeño or serrano pepper, seeded and minced

Cook until the vegetables are tender but not brown, 7 to 10 minutes. Add:

4 cloves garlic, minced
1 packed tablespoon minced peeled fresh ginger

Cook for another 2 to 3 minutes and stir in:

1 tablespoon chili powder
1 teaspoon ground cumin
½ teaspoon red pepper flakes

Cook for 1 minute and add:

2 sweet potatoes, peeled and cut into 1½-inch pieces
⅓ cup tomato paste

Salt and ground black pepper to taste

Add enough water to barely cover the vegetables and mix well. Bring to a boil, lower the heat, cover, and simmer for 45 minutes, stirring occasionally. While the stew cooks, heat in a medium skillet over high heat:

1 teaspoon peanut oil

Add:

12 ounces ground beef or turkey

Sauté, turning often, until browned. Transfer to a plate with a slotted spoon and set aside until the stew has cooked for 45 minutes. When ready, add the meat to the stew along with:

2 small zucchini (1 inch in diameter), trimmed and sliced

Cook for another 15 minutes. Place in a small bowl:

½ cup peanut butter (chunky or smooth), preferably unsalted

Stir in 1 cup of the stewing liquid until smooth and add the peanut

butter mixture to the pot. Mix well and cook another 15 minutes. Season with:

Salt and ground black pepper to taste

Serve plain (opposite) or with:

Hot cooked rice or couscous

SWEET POTATOES

When we say "sweet potatoes," we mean the ones with yellow-gray to brown skin and yellowish to white, dry, mealy flesh. Shape is not an indication of quality. All can be round or torpedo shaped, knobby or sleek. Select firm tubers with bright skin, heavy for their size, free of soft spots, dark spots, and mold. Although available year-round, the potatoes are harvested fresh fall through winter. Store sweet potatoes in a cool, dark, dry place.

ABOUT
CHOWDERS

*T*he word chowder *usually conjures up images of a steaming bowl of New England clam chowder. In nineteenth-century New England, "chowder masters," as well as home cooks, prepared versions of the soup for gatherings on the beach or at home.*

The word derives from the French chaudière, *a type of cauldron, but regional chowders have become an American culinary tradition. Early settlers made chowder from household staples: rendered salt pork was simmered in water with local fish or seafood, then thickened with sea biscuits or bread. In the nineteenth century, potatoes replaced the crackers, and milk and cream came to be added to chowder. Other milk chowders then evolved, including corn chowder. Some chowders omit the milk entirely and are tomato-based.*

New England Clam Chowder, 80

Fresh Corn Chowder

About 6 cups

Place in a soup pot and cook, stirring, over medium-low heat until it releases all of its fat and is beginning to crisp, 10 to 15 minutes:

4 slices bacon, chopped

Leaving the bacon in the pan, spoon off all but 2 tablespoons of fat. Add and cook, stirring, until tender and slightly browned, 10 to 15 minutes:

1 small onion, chopped

2 medium celery stalks, diced

Remove the kernels from:

6 small ears corn

Reserve the kernels and add the cobs to the soup pot along with:

4½ cups milk

2 medium potatoes, peeled and diced

Push the corn cobs into the milk to fully submerge them. Bring the milk to a boil. Reduce the heat and simmer, covered, until the potatoes are tender, 10 to 15 minutes. Remove the cobs. Stir in the reserved corn kernels along with:

1½ teaspoons salt

½ teaspoon ground white or black pepper

Simmer gently until the corn is tender, about 5 minutes. With a slotted spoon, remove 1½ cups solids from the soup and puree until smooth. Return to the soup and add:

1 tablespoon unsalted butter

Let stand until the butter is melted, then stir. Ladle into warmed bowls.

PREPARING CORN

In our recipes we have adopted the formula of one ear corn to equal ½ cup kernels.

To remove kernels from the cob, hold the ear firmly with the bottom end placed on a counter or in a shallow soup bowl to keep the kernels from splattering. If you want to retain the shape and texture of the whole kernel, cut straight down the cob with a sharp knife, cutting two or three rows at a time (**1**).

If you are after the inner creaminess of the kernel, cut off just the tops of the kernels. Then, with the back of your knife, scrape down the cob to press out the base of the kernels and the corn "milk," which gives body and moisture to corn purees and creamy corn dishes (**2**).

Corn Chowder with Chili Peppers

About 5 cups

A spicy, meatless corn chowder.
Heat in a soup pot, over medium-low heat until the butter is melted:

1 tablespoon unsalted butter
1 tablespoon vegetable oil

Add and cook, stirring, until tender but not browned, 5 to 10 minutes:

1 medium onion, diced
1 medium poblano pepper, seeded and diced
2 cloves garlic, minced
½ fresh jalapeño pepper, seeded and diced

Stir in:

3 cups milk
2 cups fresh corn kernels (from 2 to 3 ears)

1 teaspoon salt

Bring to a boil, reduce the heat, and simmer gently until the corn is tender, about 3 minutes. Stir in:

1 large ripe tomato, peeled, seeded, and coarsely chopped

Simmer gently for about 2 minutes to marry the flavors. With a slotted spoon, remove 1½ cups solids from the soup and puree until smooth. Return to the soup. Heat gently just to warm through. Stir in:

1 tablespoon chopped fresh cilantro

Ladle into warmed bowls. If you like, pass at the table:

Lime wedges

POBLANO PEPPER

Dark green, rich-tasting poblanos (also called pasillas) are used extensively throughout Mexico and are gaining in popularity in this country. The pepper's flesh has a compact texture with a good (but varying) amount of heat. Use them roasted and peeled in soups, sauces, and stews or whole as an edible vessel. When dried, they usually are known as ancho chilies. Poblanos measure 4 to 5 inches long and about 2½ inches wide at the stem end, tapering to a sharp point.

Manhattan Clam Chowder

About 10 cups

Salt pork, onions, seafood, potatoes, and, most of the time, milk make a traditional chowder. Manhattan clam chowder substitutes tomatoes for the milk. Some consider this blasphemy, others say it simply is not chowder, others want nothing else.

Scrub individually with a vegetable brush:

10 to 12 pounds quahogs or other hard-shell clams, preferably 2 to 3 inches across

Place in a sink or large soup pot, cover with cold water, and stir in:

¼ cup salt

Let stand for 30 minutes to rid the clams of sand. Rinse and drain in a colander. Place the clams in a large soup pot and add:

2 cups water

Cover and steam over high heat until the clams are completely open, 10 to 15 minutes. Discard any that do not open. Pour the cooking liquid through a fine-mesh sieve and set aside. When the clams are cool enough to handle, remove from the shell and chop finely. Heat in a large skillet, over medium heat:

1 tablespoon vegetable oil

Add and cook, stirring occasionally, until browned:

3 slices bacon, finely chopped

Add and cook, stirring, until tender but not browned, 5 to 10 minutes:

2 medium onions, chopped
½ green bell pepper, diced
1 large celery stalk, diced

Stir in the reserved cooking liquid along with:

One 28-ounce can whole plum tomatoes, with juice, chopped
3 cups Fish Fumet, 21, or Express Fish Broth, 28

Bring to a boil. Stir in:

1 pound potatoes, peeled and cut into 1-inch dice

Reduce the heat to medium-low and simmer until the potatoes are tender, about 20 minutes. Stir in the chopped clams and season with:

½ teaspoon ground black pepper
2 tablespoons chopped fresh parsley

Simmer briefly, then ladle into warmed bowls.

HARD-SHELL CLAMS

There are dozens of types of clams. Hard-shell clams vary more in size and color than in shape or form. All have firm, sometimes tough, meat with excellent, briny flavor. And all have the distinct advantage of being essentially free of grit. There is some confusion about nomenclature of hard-shell clams, but the common names relate primarily to size. In some areas, quahog is a generic name for hard-shells, but in others, it refers to those clams over 3 to 4 inches across. They are too tough for raw eating and too big for eating whole. Littlenecks, the smallest hard-shell, are under 2 inches across (preferably considerably under). Manila clams are about the same size. Cherrystones in some areas are 2 to 3 inches across, in others up to 4 inches. They are excellent for cooking. Mahogany clams are the same size. There are some excellent varieties that are steely gray in color.

RHODE ISLAND (PORTUGUESE-STYLE) CLAM CHOWDER

As unconventional as Manhattan clam chowder, but very tasty. Prepare Manhattan Clam Chowder, above, substituting 2 tablespoons olive oil for the bacon and adding along with the clams 6 ounces thinly sliced Portuguese linguiça or chorizo and ¼ to ½ teaspoon red pepper flakes (left). Simmer over low heat for 10 minutes. Ladle into warmed bowls.

Landlubber's Fish Chowder

12 to 14 cups; 8 to 10 servings

Use salmon, monkfish, blackfish, cod, or wolffish in this fish chowder. Flaky fish, such as flounder, mackerel, or sea bass, tend to fall apart too easily. Serve as a main course for lunch or dinner. For a reduced-fat fish chowder, omit the cream. Cream biscuits are perfect for soaking up the soup.

Remove any excess skin and, using tweezers, pick out any bones from:

3½ pounds boneless, skinless fish fillets

If you have to use a knife to cut out the bones, be sure to leave the fillets in pieces as large as possible. Place in a large soup pot and cook, stirring, over low heat until it is beginning to crisp, 10 to 15 minutes:

4 ounces meaty salt pork or 4 slices bacon, cut into ¼- to ½-inch dice

Add and cook, stirring, until the onions are tender but not browned, 10 to 15 minutes:

4 tablespoons (½ stick) unsalted butter

2 large onions, cut into 1-inch dice

3 bay leaves

1 tablespoon chopped fresh thyme

Stir in:

3 large Maine or other boiling potatoes, peeled, halved lengthwise, and cut into ¼-inch-thick slices

3 cups Fish Stock, 21, Fish Fumet, 21, or Express Fish Broth, 28

Bring to a boil, reduce the heat, and simmer until the potatoes are tender, about 20 minutes. Remove the bay leaves and stir in the fish fillets along with:

2 cups heavy cream

Simmer until the fish is cooked through and beginning to flake, 8 to 10 minutes. Season with:

Salt and ground black pepper to taste

2 tablespoons chopped fresh parsley and/or chervil

Remove from the heat. Ladle into soup dishes. Top each serving with:

Dollop of butter

Serve with:

Cream Biscuits, 123, or common crackers

New England Clam Chowder

About 4 cups

This New England clam chowder gets its creamy thickness from heavy cream and the starch in the potatoes.

Scrub individually with a vegetable brush:

5 pounds quahogs or other hard-shell clams

Place in a sink or large soup pot, cover with cold water, and stir in:

¼ cup salt

Let stand for 30 minutes to rid the clams of sand. Rinse and drain in a colander. Place the clams in a large soup pot and add:

1 cup water

Any scraps of onion, celery, thyme, or bay leaf (optional)

Cover and steam over high heat until the clams are completely open, 10 to 15 minutes. Discard any that do not open. Pour the cooking liquid through a fine-mesh sieve and set aside. When the clams are cool enough to handle, remove from their shells and coarsely chop into ⅜-inch pieces.

Place in a soup pot and cook, stirring, over medium heat until slightly crisp:

2 slices bacon or 2 ounces salt pork, diced

Stir in:

1 medium onion, cut into ½-inch dice

1 bay leaf

1½ teaspoons chopped fresh thyme

1 tablespoon unsalted butter

When the onions are translucent, add the reserved cooking liquid along with:

3 red or white new potatoes, cut into ½-inch dice

Bring to a boil, reduce the heat, and simmer until the potatoes are tender, about 12 minutes. Stir in the chopped clams along with:

1 cup heavy cream

Simmer for 5 minutes. Season with:

Ground black pepper to taste

1 tablespoon chopped fresh parsley

Ladle into soup dishes or cups.

Serve with:

Cream Biscuits, 123, or common crackers

Pacific Northwest Salmon Chowder

About 5 cups

In a small saucepan, simmer, whisking occasionally, until reduced to ⅔ cup:

1 cup heavy cream

Meanwhile, melt in a soup pot over medium heat:

1 tablespoon unsalted butter

Add and cook, stirring, until the leeks are tender but not browned, 5 to 10 minutes:

2 medium leeks (white part only), cleaned and chopped

¼ cup dry vermouth
1 clove garlic, minced

Stir in:

3 cups Fish Stock, 21, Fish Fumet, 21, or Express Fish Broth, 28
2 red or white new potatoes, diced
½ teaspoon salt

Bring to a boil, reduce the heat, and simmer until the potatoes are cooked, 10 to 15 minutes. Reduce the heat to low. Add the reduced cream along with:

1 salmon fillet (about 12 ounces)
¼ teaspoon ground black or white pepper

Simmer just until the salmon is cooked, 8 to 10 minutes, depending on the thickness of the fish. Gently break apart the fillet with a wooden spoon. Serve immediately, garnished with:

Small dill sprigs

ABOUT
FISH AND
SEAFOOD
SOUPS & STEWS

*F*ish and seafood lend themselves to soups and stews, because they stay moist and tender when cooked at a low temperature and closely watched. But they are easy to overcook, so serve or remove from the heat as soon as the fish is cooked. A light chicken stock is often a better substitute for fish fumet than many commercial fish or clam broths, which may add a fishy taste to the soup. With the exception of most chowders, which tend to sit well overnight, generally fish soups are best eaten as soon as they are cooked.

Bouillabaisse, 86

Cream of Mussel Soup (Billi Bi)

About 4 cups

This is a French mussel soup made with cream and white wine. The secret to this soup is to strain the mussel cooking liquid through several layers of cheesecloth to make sure you trap every possible grain of sand. You will find the optional curry powder at the end to be a perfect accent against the creamy broth.

Scrub individually with a vegetable brush:

3 pounds small mussels

Remove the beards. Discard any damaged mussels or those that do not close with a sharp tap on the counter. Place the mussels in a large soup pot along with:

1½ cups dry white wine
⅓ cup chopped shallots
5 sprigs fresh parsley
3 sprigs fresh thyme

Cover and steam over medium heat until the mussels are completely open. Discard any that do not open. Pour the cooking liquid through a sieve lined with several layers of dampened cheesecloth or paper towels into a medium saucepan. Bring to a low simmer. When the mussels are cool enough to handle, remove from their shells. Whisk together in a small bowl:

1 cup heavy cream or half-and-half
1 large egg yolk

Gradually whisk about 1 cup of the cooking liquid into the egg mixture, then whisk back into the saucepan. Heat gently, but do not boil.

Season with:

Salt to taste
Pinch of ground red or white pepper
½ teaspoon curry powder (optional)

Ladle into warmed bowls. Garnish with the reserved mussels and sprinkle with:

Snipped fresh chives

MUSSELS

Blue mussels are the most common variety. New Zealand green-lipped mussels are also good and can be used interchangeably. The quality of mussels is difficult to judge in the store, and their meat is firm, plump, large, sweet, and clean at its best. You can be certain you are buying live mussels, but you cannot be certain you are buying delicious ones. A wise policy is to identify the source when you have good mussels and try to stay with it. Many retailers buy their mussels from the same source over and over, and they can be consistently fine. Some mussels are farm-raised, and their advocates claim that these are more consistent than wild mussels. Some mussel shells are beautifully clean and shiny; others are encrusted with barnacles and other evidence of life at sea. Neither is an indication of quality. Like clams and oysters, mussels must be alive (or cooked) at the time of purchase. The smell should be appealing and the shell intact. Reject any with broken shells or those that seem unusually light or heavy (they may be empty or filled with mud). Gaping is okay, but live mussels will close—slowly but surely—when you squeeze or tap the shell.

To clean mussels, remove the "beard," the hairy vegetative growth attached to the shell. You can usually just tug it off or cut it with a knife. Wash the mussels in several changes of cold water (if time allows, place them in a pot and run a slow stream of cold water over them for an hour, no longer). Keep washing until the water runs clear. Sort through the mussels and discard any with damaged shells. Be sure not to store mussels in a sealed plastic bag. They will suffocate. Store preferably in a bowl or mesh bag, in the refrigerator, covered lightly with a damp towel. Ice is not necessary; mollusks will stay alive for days at 40°F.

Oyster Stew

About 4 cups

This dish comes together quickly. A double boiler prevents overcooking of the oysters. In many New England homes, this is often served before the turkey at Thanksgiving, but there is no need to wait for a holiday to enjoy this stew.

Combine in the top of a double boiler set directly over medium-low heat:

2 to 4 tablespoons unsalted butter

1 tablespoon or more grated onions or leeks, a sliver of garlic, or ½ cup minced celery

Cook, stirring, until the butter is melted and the onions are tender but not browned, about 5 minutes. Stir in:

1 to 1½ pints shucked oysters, with their liquor

1½ cups milk

½ cup light cream

½ teaspoon salt

⅛ teaspoon ground white pepper or sweet or hot paprika

Place the top of the double boiler over, not in, boiling water. When the milk is hot and the oysters are floating, stir in:

2 tablespoons chopped fresh parsley

Ladle into warmed bowls.

OYSTER BISQUE

This is a delicious bisque for oyster lovers. Temper the egg yolks to prevent them from scrambling with a small amount of the stew before adding them to the pot.

Prepare *Oyster Stew, left,* but before adding the parsley, remove the stew from the heat and pour a small quantity over 2 beaten egg yolks. After mixing, add them slowly to the hot stew. Heat over low heat for 1 minute, but do not allow to boil. Serve immediately.

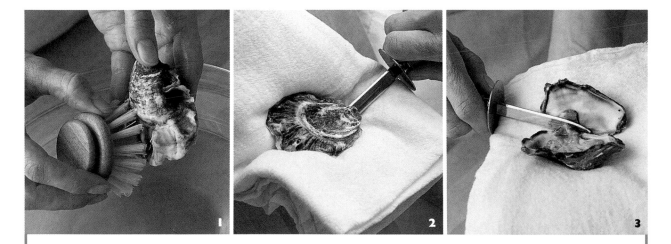

HOW TO CLEAN AND SHUCK OYSTERS

1 To clean oysters, use a stiff brush and scrub the shells thoroughly, in particular the often-encrusted Eastern and European oysters (Pacific oysters tend to be cleaner).

2 To shuck oysters, hold the oyster, deep shell down, firmly in a folded kitchen towel over a bowl. Insert the point of an oyster knife, which has a strong pointed blade and protective shield, into the hinge between the shells at the pointed end of the oyster. Turn the knife to pry open the oyster and lift the upper shell enough to cut through the hinge muscle. Run the knife point between the shells to open the oyster.

3 Once open, scrape the oyster from its shell, but do not remove it. To serve the oysters raw, nestle the shells in some ice or rock salt. Strain any liquor (oyster liquid) in the bowl and pour it over the oysters. To cook the oysters, remove them to a measuring cup or bowl. Strain the liquor and reserve it for cooking.

Bouillabaisse

About 8 cups; 4 to 6 servings

In this classic Provençal fisherman's stew, the only rule is that it should be a mix of different kinds of fish and shellfish paired with a combination of garlic, tomato, saffron, and fennel. The seafood suggestions in this recipe are only a guide. Well-scrubbed clams, mussels, shrimp, all in the shell, can be added, as can a number of fish types: snapper, halibut, and perch, to name a few. Remember that bouillabaisse should capture the flavor of the freshest catch of the day, and need not adhere to strict rules.

Heat in a large saucepan, over medium heat until the butter is melted:

1 tablespoon olive oil

1 tablespoon unsalted butter

Add and cook, stirring occasionally, until the vegetables are tender but not browned, 5 to 10 minutes:

1 medium leek (white and green parts), cleaned thoroughly, halved lengthwise, and cut into ½-inch pieces

1 small fennel bulb, quartered, cored, and thinly sliced

1 medium celery stalk, cut into thin diagonal slices

1 bay leaf

1 star anise, or ¼ teaspoon anise seeds or fennel seeds (optional)

Peel of ½ orange (optional)

¼ teaspoon saffron threads

½ teaspoon salt

Add:

3 cloves garlic, minced

Cook, stirring, for 2 minutes more. Reduce the heat if the bottom begins to scorch. Add:

1 tablespoon tomato paste

Cook, stirring, for 1 minute. Stir in:

½ cup dry white wine

Bring to a gentle boil and cook for 3 minutes. Stir in:

1½ cups canned whole tomatoes, with juice, broken into pieces

2 cups *Fish Stock*, 21, *Fish Fumet*, 21, or *Express Fish Broth*, 28

½ teaspoon ground red pepper

¾ teaspoon salt

Bring to a boil, reduce the heat, cover, and simmer for 20 minutes. The bouillabaisse broth can be made a day in advance.

Bring to the smoking point in a large soup pot over high heat:

2 tablespoons olive oil

Add:

12 littleneck or other small clams, well scrubbed

Cook, stirring, for 2 to 3 minutes. Keep the oil from smoking. Remove the star anise and orange peel if using, and add the reserved broth. Bring to a boil, reduce the heat, and simmer for 3 minutes. Stir in:

¾ pound monkfish, sea bass, red snapper, or halibut fillets, or a combination, cut into 1½-inch pieces

Continue to cook, covered, for 1 minute. Stir in:

12 sea scallops (about ½ pound)

Cook just until the seafood is done, 2 to 3 minutes more. Discard any clams that are not open. Stir in:

2 tablespoons Pernod (optional)

Serve with:

***Croutons*, 124**

***Saffron Garlic Mayonnaise*, 119**

Bourride of Monkfish and Clams

About 8 cups

This is a modern take on the classic fish soup from Provence. In honoring the dish's origins, we have stirred the local mayonnaise (aïoli) right into the fish broth. This is an easy dish to prepare and a great dish for company. Shell the clams for a more elegant presentation or arrange them in their shells over the top of the bourride.

Heat in a large nonreactive skillet over medium-high heat:

¼ cup olive oil

Have ready:

2 pounds monkfish fillets, cut into 2 x 1-inch pieces

Sprinkle with:

Ground black pepper to taste

Place the fish in the skillet in an even layer and cook until browned on one side, 5 to 7 minutes. Turn the monkfish over and stir in:

24 littleneck or other small clams, well scrubbed

3 medium leeks (white and tender green parts), cleaned thoroughly and cut crosswise into ¼-inch-thick slices

1 teaspoon chopped fresh thyme

¼ teaspoon saffron threads

Pinch of red pepper flakes

1½ cups dry white wine

Cover the skillet, reduce the heat to medium, and cook until the clams are completely open, 8 to 15 minutes. Discard any that do not open. Remove from the heat and remove the clams from the skillet. Shell the clams and return them to the skillet.

If leaving clams in the shell, add them. Add:

1 cup *Garlic Mayonnaise* (Aïoli), 118, using the larger amount of garlic

Gently shake the skillet and stir the sauce with a wooden spoon until it is thickened and coats the fish and clams. Stir in:

1 teaspoon fresh lemon juice

Season with:

Ground black pepper to taste

Ladle into warmed shallow bowls and sprinkle with:

1 tablespoon chopped fresh parsley

Pass separately to float atop the soup:

Garlic croutons

Louisiana Court Bouillon

About 7 cups

A court bouillon is a light-flavored broth used for cooking food, primarily fish, but also vegetables and meat. This is not a classic court bouillon but a spicy Cajun fish and tomato stew. Redfish or snapper is often used in this dish, but you can use any white flaky fish. We have added shrimp, but feel free to omit or to add your favorite shellfish.

Heat in a large skillet over medium heat:

3 tablespoons vegetable oil

Add and cook, stirring, until lightly browned, about 5 minutes:

3 tablespoons all-purpose flour

Add and cook, stirring, just until softened, about 3 minutes:

½ cup diced green bell peppers
½ cup diced celery
½ cup diced onions
2 cloves garlic, minced
½ teaspoon dried thyme

Stir in:

One 28-ounce can whole plum tomatoes, drained and coarsely chopped
2 cups *Fish Stock*, 21, *Fish Fumet*, 21, or *Express Fish Broth*, 28

Bring to a boil, reduce the heat to medium-low, and simmer for 10 minutes. Stir in:

1 pound flaky white fish fillets (such as haddock or snapper), cut into 2-inch pieces

12 small shrimp (about ¼ pound), peeled and deveined

Cover and cook until the fish is opaque in the center, about 3 minutes. Season with:

2 teaspoons Worcestershire sauce
1 teaspoon salt
¾ to 1¼ teaspoons hot red pepper sauce

Stir in:

½ to ¾ cup cooked long-grain rice

Taste and adjust the seasonings, adding more Worcestershire and hot red pepper sauce as desired. Ladle into warmed bowls.

Charleston Crab Soup

About 4 cups

Whole blue crabs are sold in markets. They are a nuisance to clean and pick yourself; the yield is somewhere between 10 and 15 percent (you would have to pick 7 to 10 crabs to obtain 1 pound of meat) and, unless you are highly skilled, each crab will take you about 10 minutes to clean. So if you want meat for recipes, buy prepicked, fresh—not pasteurized—lump crabmeat. This elegant soup is called she-crab soup when made with female crabs and their roe.

Melt in a large saucepan, over low heat:

3 tablespoons unsalted butter

Whisk in:

3 tablespoons all-purpose flour

Cook, whisking, until the flour smells toasted but is not browned, about 3 minutes. Gradually whisk in:

3 cups milk
1 teaspoon Worcestershire sauce
¾ teaspoon hot red pepper sauce

Bring to a boil, whisking, reduce the heat, and simmer for about 5 minutes. Reduce the heat to low and stir in:

1 pound lump crabmeat, picked over for shells and cartilage, with roe if available
1 to 2 tablespoons dry sherry
¾ teaspoon salt

Taste and adjust the seasonings, adding more hot red pepper sauce if desired. Heat gently just until the crab is warmed through. Ladle into warmed bowls. Garnish with:

Thinly sliced scallion greens

HANDLING FISH AT HOME

Refrigerators are not cold enough to store fish, which keeps almost twice as well at 32° or 33°F as it does at 40°F, the temperature of most refrigerators. Fill the vegetable bin or a baking pan with ice (or ice packs) and bury your wrapped fish in there. Although some fish will retain their quality for as long as ten days, many of those days are spent in getting the fish from the water to your home. Even a farm-raised fish is probably at least three days old by the time it reaches your supermarket counter. So it makes the most sense to buy fish the day you are going to eat it, or at most the day before.

Caribbean Callaloo

About 12 cups

Callaloo is the name given to a family of plants favored in the Caribbean for their tart green leaves. Callaloo leaves are occasionally found canned in Caribbean markets, but fresh spinach and Swiss chard are good substitutes. Canned callaloo leaves cook more quickly than fresh. The soup includes okra, which should not be cooked in an aluminum, iron, or unlined copper pot. This soup can also be served over rice as a hearty main course.

Place in a soup pot and cook, stirring, over medium heat until almost crisp:

3 slices bacon, thinly sliced crosswise

Leaving the bacon in the pot, pour off all but 1 teaspoon of the fat and add:

8 ounces ham, cubed
1 medium onion, chopped
1 clove garlic, minced
3 scallions, thinly sliced

Cook, stirring, until the onions are tender but not browned, 5 to 10 minutes.

Stir in:

1 pound callaloo, spinach, or Swiss chard, trimmed, washed, dried, and coarsely chopped
5 cups *Chicken Stock*, 22
¼ teaspoon dried thyme

Cover, bring to a boil, and simmer for 5 minutes. Reduce the heat, remove the cover, and add:

8 ounces lump crabmeat, picked over for shells and cartilage, or sliced raw shrimp
8 ounces white fish fillets (such as tilefish, cod, grouper, or sea bass), cooked or raw
½ teaspoon salt
8 ounces fresh okra, sliced, or frozen sliced okra
1 cup unsweetened coconut milk
Ground black pepper to taste

Simmer until the okra and fish are cooked, about 10 minutes. The fillets will break up as they cook. Serve immediately.

Thai Clam Pot

4 to 6 servings

Here are clams at their spiciest and most delicious.

Have ready:

8 cloves garlic, thinly slivered

8 scallions, cut into 2-inch lengths, then lengthwise in half

1 teaspoon red pepper flakes

1 cup rice wine mixed with 1 cup water

3 pounds small littleneck clams, well washed and drained

1 cup fresh basil leaves, cut into thin strips

2 tablespoons fish sauce

When ready to cook, bring to a rolling boil in a large pot:

12 to 16 cups water

Add and cook until done, 2 to 3 minutes:

4 ounces thin somen noodles or angel-hair pasta

Drain immediately in a sieve and rinse lightly to remove starch. While the noodles are cooking, heat a heavy pot large enough to hold the clams over high heat until hot. Add:

2 tablespoons peanut oil

Heat, swirling, until very hot but not smoking. Add the garlic, scallions, and red pepper flakes. Stir for about 15 seconds. Standing back, add the wine mixture, cover, and bring to a boil. Add the clams, cover, and return the liquid to a boil. Immediately reduce the heat to medium and cook until the clams have just opened, 7 to 8 minutes, shaking the pot 3 or 4 times to ensure that the clams cook evenly.

Add the basil and stir it thoroughly into the liquid. Cover and cook for 30 to 45 seconds. Add the fish sauce and stir thoroughly. Divide the noodles among individual bowls, add the clams, and pour the broth over them. Serve immediately.

Sardinian Seafood Stew (Cassola)

About 8 cups; 4 to 6 servings

Soak in a small amount of hot water to cover for 30 minutes:

5 sun-dried tomato halves, preferably packed in oil

Drain and reserve the soaking liquid. Chop the tomatoes and reserve. Scrub individually with a vegetable brush:

1 pound small mussels

Remove the beards. Discard any damaged mussels or those that do not close with a sharp tap on the counter. Place the mussels in a large soup pot, along with:

1 cup dry white wine

Cover the pot, place it over high heat, and cook, shaking the pot occasionally, until most of the mussels are opened, about 10 minutes. Discard any mussels that have not opened. Lift the mussels from the pot and remove most of them from their shells, but reserve a few in the shells for garnish. Continue to cook the cooking liquid until reduced to about 1 cup. Pour through a sieve lined with several layers of dampened cheesecloth or paper towels, and set aside. Place in a large saucepan along with the drained sun-dried tomatoes:

1 tablespoon olive oil
1 medium onion, chopped
½ cup chopped fresh basil

Cook, stirring, over medium heat until the onions are golden, 10 to 15 minutes. Add:

½ pound squid, cleaned and cut into bite-sized pieces

Increase the heat to high and cook, stirring almost constantly, until the squid begins to brown, 3 to 4 minutes. Add the reserved tomato soaking liquid along with:

1 teaspoon minced garlic
1 dried red chili pepper

Cook, stirring, until the liquid is evaporated, about 2 minutes. Stir in the reserved mussel cooking liquid along with:

3 cups chopped, seeded, peeled tomatoes, fresh or canned

2 cups Fish Stock, 21, Fish Fumet, 21, Express Fish Broth, 28, or water

Bring to a boil, reduce the heat to medium-low, and simmer, stirring occasionally, until the squid is tender, about 1 hour. Remove the chili pepper and stir in:

2 tablespoons red wine vinegar

Add:

1 pound shrimp, peeled, deveined, if desired
1 pound firm white-fleshed fish fillets or steaks, such as snapper, halibut, grouper, or monkfish

Cover and cook until the fish is tender, 5 to 10 minutes. The fish fillets will break up as they cook. Add the shelled mussels to the pot and cook just until heated through. Season with:

Salt and ground black pepper to taste

Garnish with the reserved mussels in their shells and sprinkle with:

Minced fresh parsley

Serve with:

Crusty French bread

Lobster Bisque

About 8 cups

A classic lobster bisque derives its deep flavor and dusky-pink color from beef stock and its distinctive, velvety body from rice. The soup should be thick but not too thick, so thin it as necessary before serving.

Combine in a wide, deep pot or Dutch oven and bring to a boil over high heat:

5 cups water

2 cups dry white wine

2 cups Fish Stock, 21, or Fish Fumet, 21

1 cup Classic Beef Stock, 24, or Brown Beef Stock, 24

Place in the pot back side down:

2 live lobsters (1¼ to 1½ pounds each)

Cover the pot tightly, return the liquid to a boil, and cook for 6 minutes. Turn the lobsters with tongs, cover the pot, and cook for 6 minutes more. Remove from the heat. Remove the lobsters from the broth. When cool enough to handle, remove the meat from the shells and discard the coral and green matter (tomalley). Cover and refrigerate the meat. Chop the shells and bodies, return to the broth, and simmer, uncovered, for 45 minutes. Strain through a fine-mesh sieve and discard the solids. You need 6 cups of broth. If you have more, boil it over high heat until reduced to 6 cups. If you have less, add water to make 6 cups. Melt in a large saucepan over medium heat:

3 to 4 tablespoons unsalted butter

Add and cook, stirring, until tender but not browned, 5 to 10 minutes:

1 cup finely chopped onions

⅓ cup finely chopped carrots

⅓ cup finely chopped celery

Stir in the 6 cups of broth along with:

1½ cups chopped, seeded, peeled tomatoes, fresh or canned

⅓ cup long-grain rice

1 bay leaf

1½ teaspoons minced fresh tarragon, or ½ teaspoon dried

1 teaspoon sweet or hot paprika

½ teaspoon minced garlic

½ teaspoon salt

¼ teaspoon dried thyme

⅛ teaspoon ground red pepper

Bring to a boil, reduce the heat, and simmer, partially covered, for 40 minutes. Meanwhile, cut the lobster meat into ¼-inch dice. Melt in a medium skillet over medium heat:

2 to 4 tablespoons unsalted butter

Add the lobster meat and cook, stirring, until heated through. Stir in:

¼ cup Cognac or brandy

¼ teaspoon salt

¼ teaspoon ground white pepper, preferably freshly ground

Cook, stirring, until nearly all of the liquid is evaporated. Set aside ⅓ cup of the meat for garnish. Add the rest of the meat and any juices to the soup mixture. Remove the bay leaf. In a food processor or, preferably, a blender, puree the soup in small batches until smooth. Return the soup to the saucepan and stir in the reserved lobster meat along with:

½ to 1 cup heavy cream

Heat the bisque through over low heat. Thin, if necessary, with:

Clam broth or milk

Remove from the heat and season with:

Drops of fresh lemon juice to taste

Salt and ground white pepper to taste

Ground red pepper to taste

If you wish, garnish each serving with:

2 tablespoons minced fresh tarragon or parsley

LOBSTERS

Lobsters fall neatly into two groups: those with claws and those without. Those with claws—on this continent commonly called Maine lobster even when taken from Canada or elsewhere on the North Atlantic coast—are generally agreed to be superior and are, in fact, true lobsters. Those without, which have excellent tail meat, most often are seen locally (in Florida, the Gulf States, and southern California) or in the form of frozen lobster tails. European lobsters never make it to this side of the Atlantic. All lobsters can be used interchangeably in recipes, although those without claws obviously have less meat than those with claws.

SHRIMP BISQUE

This bisque is a delightful treat. Prepare *Lobster Bisque, opposite,* substituting 1 pound shell-on shrimp for the lobsters. Steam the shrimp until the shells turn pink and curl, about 2 minutes, and simmer the shells for only 30 minutes.

ABOUT
MEAT AND
POULTRY
SOUPS & STEWS

*M*any of these robust soups and stews can be served as a full meal. All the meat soups here require long simmering. This allows economical cuts of meat to become tender and impart their full flavor to the soup or stew.

Tough but flavorful stewing hens are difficult to find, so the poultry soups and stews in this section are made with chicken. Because chicken cooks fast, it is easy to prepare substantial soup or stew quickly. All chicken, especially white meat, becomes dry and stringy with overcooking. So reheat the soup or stew gently, just until hot. Improvise your own versions with seasonal ingredients on hand.

Chicken Gumbo, 99

Beef Stew

6 to 8 servings

Pat dry:

2 pounds boneless stewing beef, such as chuck, short-rib meat, or bottom round, cut into 2-inch cubes

Season the meat with:

½ to 1 teaspoon dried herbs (thyme, marjoram, savory, oregano, and/or basil)

½ teaspoon salt

½ teaspoon ground black pepper

Dredge the meat with:

½ cup all-purpose flour

Shake off any excess flour. Heat in a Dutch oven over medium-high heat:

2 tablespoons olive or vegetable oil, bacon fat, beef drippings, or other fat

Add the meat in batches and brown on all sides, being careful not to crowd the pan or scorch the meat. Remove with a slotted spoon. Pour off all but 2 tablespoons of fat from the pan (add more if needed). Add:

½ cup chopped onions

¼ cup chopped carrots

¼ cup chopped celery

¼ cup chopped leeks (optional)

2 tablespoons chopped garlic (optional)

Cover and cook, stirring often, over medium heat until the onions are softened, about 5 minutes. Add:

2 bay leaves

½ to 1 teaspoon of the same herbs used to season the meat

½ teaspoon salt

½ teaspoon ground black pepper

Add enough to cover the meat at least halfway:

2 to 3 cups *Beef Stock*, 24, or *Chicken Stock*, 22, dry red or white wine, or beer

Bring to a boil. Reduce the heat, cover, and simmer over low heat until the meat is fork-tender, 1½ to 2 hours. Add:

2 to 3 carrots, peeled and cut into 1-inch chunks

3 or 4 boiling potatoes, peeled and cut into 1-inch chunks

2 turnips, peeled and cut into 1-inch chunks

2 parsnips, peeled and cut into 1-inch chunks

Cover and cook until the vegetables are tender, 35 to 40 minutes. Remove the pan from the heat and skim off any fat from the surface. Taste and adjust the seasonings. If you wish, thicken the sauce by stirring together and whisking into the stew:

1 to 1½ tablespoons *Kneaded Butter*, below

Simmer, stirring, until thickened. Garnish with:

Chopped fresh parsley

Kneaded Butter

About 2 tablespoons

Known as beurre manié *in French, kneaded butter is a convenient last-minute thickener, added to a cooked liquid just before serving. Kneaded butter is simply softened butter mixed with an equal proportion of flour and kneaded by hand or with a fork. It is shaped into balls the size of a pea that can be whisked into a simmering liquid. Once you have* added the butter, bring the liquid back to a simmer and remove the pan from the heat; extended cooking or boiling may cause the liquid to separate. Since the flour is not cooked, it can leave a raw flour taste, so use kneaded butter sparingly.

Knead together by hand or with a fork:

1 tablespoon softened butter

1 tablespoon flour

Borscht

About 8 cups

This is the original Russian borscht, meaty and brimming with tomatoes and cabbage. The beets are roasted instead of boiled, for added flavor.

Preheat the oven to 400°F.
Scrub:

12 ounces beets

Wrap the beets together in aluminum foil and roast on a baking sheet until they can easily be pierced with a fork, about 1 hour. Let cool, peel, then slice and cut into thin strips.

While the beets are roasting, prepare:

1 pound boneless beef chuck, cubed, or 1½ pounds pork spareribs, cut into single ribs

Lightly dredge with:

All-purpose flour

Heat in a soup pot, over medium-high heat:

2 tablespoons vegetable oil

Add the meat and brown on all sides. Stir in:

4½ cups *Brown Beef Stock, 24,* or water

One 28-ounce can whole plum tomatoes, drained and chopped

Bring to a boil, reduce the heat, and simmer, partially covered, until the meat is almost tender, about 30 minutes. Stir in:

2 cups shredded green or red cabbage

1 medium onion, chopped

2 medium carrots, peeled and sliced

2 medium celery stalks, sliced

1½ teaspoons tomato paste

Simmer, partially covered, until the vegetables and meat are tender, about 30 minutes. Stir in the beets along with:

2 tablespoons red wine vinegar

2 teaspoons fresh lemon juice

2 cloves garlic, minced

½ teaspoon salt, or to taste

¾ teaspoon ground black pepper

1½ teaspoons sugar (optional)

Simmer, partially covered, for 15 minutes. Thin the soup with water if necessary. Ladle into warmed bowls. Garnish with:

Sour cream
Snipped fresh dill

Scotch Broth

About 6 cups

Funny how barley, a crop traced back to 7000 B.C., continues to surprise and delight today, as if every dish it appears in reinvents its roasted-nut taste. The off-white oval kernels most commonly sold as pearl barley have had the tough husk, bran, and germ ground away, yielding the endosperm, a kernel that cooks much faster than hulled, or whole, barley. This Scottish classic is hundreds of years old in origin and is known for its use of barley and lamb.

Bring to a boil in a soup pot:

6 cups water

1½ pounds lamb shoulder, trimmed of fat and cut into ½-inch pieces

Reduce the heat, and simmer for 10 minutes. Skim the impurities from the surface. Stir in:

½ cup pearl barley

3 medium leeks (white part only), cleaned thoroughly and chopped

1 large carrot, peeled and diced

1 large celery stalk, diced

½ teaspoon salt

Bring to a boil, reduce the heat, and simmer, partially covered, until the meat is tender, about 1½ hours. Replenish the water as needed. Spoon off the fat from the surface and season with:

Salt and ground black pepper to taste

2 tablespoons chopped fresh parsley

Pennsylvania Dutch Chicken Corn Soup

About 6 cups

Use any type of wide egg noodle you like in this chicken corn soup. Some recipes call for a garnish of popcorn to reinforce the corn flavor and to add some crunch to the soup.

Bring to a boil in a soup pot:

**6 cups water, or 3 cups water and
    3 cups Chicken Stock, 22**

**1½ to 2 pounds chicken parts, or
    ½ whole chicken, cut into
    serving pieces**

**1 teaspoon salt (½ teaspoon if
    using chicken stock)**

⅛ teaspoon ground black pepper

Skim the impurities from the surface. Reduce the heat and simmer, covered, until the chicken is well cooked, about 1 hour. Remove the chicken, discard the skin and bones, shred the meat, and set aside. (At this point you can remove the surface fat with a small ladle.)

Bring the stock to a boil. Stir in:

1¾ cups short, wide egg noodles

1 cup fresh or frozen corn kernels

Cook, stirring occasionally, until the noodles are tender but firm. Stir in the shredded chicken along with:

1 hard-boiled egg, chopped

**1½ tablespoons chopped fresh
    parsley**

Ladle into warmed bowls.

Chicken Gumbo

About 10 cups

Quingombo, *an African Congo word for okra, became "gumbo" in Louisiana and came to be known as a thick soup/stew thickened either with okra or with filé powder (ground sassafras root). This version of chicken gumbo gets its distinctive taste from a wonderful dark roux of oil and flour and a mix of dried spices. Make this recipe a day or two ahead if you can, for it only improves with time.*

Combine in a small bowl
and reserve:

½ cup chopped celery
½ cup chopped onions
½ cup chopped green bell peppers

Combine in a large plastic or
paper bag:

2 teaspoons ground red pepper
1½ teaspoons salt
1 teaspoon ground black pepper
1 teaspoon garlic powder

Add and shake until completely
covered:

1 whole chicken (about 3 pounds),
cut into serving pieces

Add and shake again:

½ cup all-purpose flour

Heat in a large cast-iron or other
skillet over medium heat:

2 to 4 tablespoons vegetable oil

Add and brown the chicken pieces
on all sides, 5 to 10 minutes.
Remove and set aside. Add to
the skillet, scraping up the
browned bits:

½ cup vegetable oil

Whisk in:

½ cup all-purpose flour

Cook, stirring often, over medium-low heat until the roux turns reddish brown, 5 to 6 minutes. Gently stir with a long-handled wooden spoon, using caution, because the roux is extremely hot and sticks to the skin. (If black specks appear, the roux is burned—so begin again in a clean pot.) Remove from the heat, add the reserved vegetables, and stir until the roux stops bubbling, 1 to 2 minutes. Carefully add the roux and vegetable mixture to a soup pot.

Whisk in:

8 cups Chicken Stock, 22, or Brown
Chicken Stock, 22

Bring to a boil, whisking. Reduce the heat and add the chicken. Simmer until the chicken is cooked through, about 30 to 45 minutes. Remove the chicken from the pot and discard the skin and bones, shred the meat, and reserve. Stir into the soup pot:

12 ounces andouille or chorizo
sausage, cut into thin slices or
small cubes
1 tablespoon chopped garlic

Simmer until the sausage is cooked through, about 10 minutes. Stir in the reserved chicken meat along with:

½ cup chopped scallions
Salt to taste
Hot red pepper sauce to taste

Ladle into warmed bowls. Garnish with:

Sliced scallion greens

Puerto Rican Chicken Rice Soup (Asopao de Pollo)

About 9 cups

This dish is traditionally made with annatto seeds, which give the soup its characteristically yellow color; this recipe uses ground annatto, but it can be omitted. Serve this soup/stew as soon as it cooks, before the rice absorbs the broth.

Combine:

1½ teaspoons garlic powder
1½ teaspoons onion powder
1½ teaspoons dried oregano
¾ teaspoon salt
¾ teaspoon ground black pepper

Rub the spice mixture, known as adobo seasoning, into the skin of:

1 whole chicken (about 3 pounds), cut into serving pieces

Heat in a soup pot, over medium-low heat:

3 tablespoons vegetable oil

Add and cook, stirring, until tender but not browned, 5 to 10 minutes:

1 medium onion, diced
1 medium green bell pepper, diced
½ cup diced ham
1 Scotch bonnet pepper or 2 fresh jalapeño peppers, seeded and diced
2 cloves garlic, minced

Stir in the chicken along with:

6 cups water
One 14½-ounce can diced tomatoes, drained
2 teaspoons ground annatto seeds (optional)

Bring to a boil, reduce the heat, and simmer, partially covered, for 25 minutes. Stir in:

½ cup long-grain rice

Continue to simmer until the chicken and rice are cooked, about 20 minutes. Remove the chicken, discard the skin and bones, and shred the meat. Return it to the soup and stir in:

1 cup fresh or frozen peas
½ cup chopped fresh cilantro
½ cup pimiento strips or sliced green olives stuffed with pimientos
Salt to taste

Simmer gently until the peas are just cooked through, 2 to 3 minutes. Ladle into warmed bowls.

Thai Chicken and Coconut Soup

About 6 cups

Coconut milk is an infusion of grated coconut and boiling water or milk and is easily made from scratch. Pour 1 cup boiling water or milk over 1 packed cup fresh coconut shreds. Stir well, cover, and let steep for 30 minutes. Process the mixture (no more than 3 cups at a time) in a blender or food processor for 1 minute. Pour all the shreds and milk into a damp clean cloth and press the liquid into a bowl, squeezing until the shreds are dry. The first pressing is referred to as thick coconut milk, and the yield is about 1 cup. Cover, refrigerate, and use within 3 days. Simmer kaffir lime leaves or lemon grass in the coconut milk first for a delicate citrus flavor.

Bring to a boil in a soup pot:

3 cups Chicken Stock, 22

2⅔ cups unsweetened coconut milk

Reduce the heat and stir in:

2 small Thai peppers or 3 fresh jalapeño peppers, seeded and sliced
3 tablespoons Thai fish sauce (nam pla) or soy sauce
1 teaspoon minced peeled fresh ginger
⅛ teaspoon salt

Simmer for 10 minutes, then stir in:

1 pound boneless, skinless chicken breasts, thinly sliced
2 tablespoons fresh lime juice

Simmer, stirring occasionally, until the chicken is no longer pink, about 5 minutes. Ladle into warmed bowls. Garnish with:

Chopped fresh cilantro

FISH SAUCE

Called nu'o'c ma'm in Vietnam and nam pla in Thailand, fish sauce is made by packing fish, usually anchovies, in crocks or barrels, covering them with brine, and allowing them to ferment in the tropical sun over a period of months. The resulting brown liquid is drained off and used. The first siphoning is most highly prized and is usually reserved for dipping sauces. Fish sauce keeps indefinitely on the shelf.

Chicken Soup Cockaigne

About 10 cups

This soup has a few surprises. The sweet taste of parsnips adds a wonderful note, as does the ground mace. Vary the vegetables and substitute ¼ cup rice or 2 ounces egg noodles for the potatoes, if desired.

Bring to a boil in a soup pot:

8 cups Chicken Stock, 22

1 whole chicken (about 3 pounds), cut into serving pieces, or 3 pounds chicken parts

3 large carrots, diced

3 parsnips or 2 small purple-top turnips, peeled and diced (optional)

3 large celery stalks, diced

3 medium onions, coarsely chopped

2 medium leeks (white part only), cleaned thoroughly and sliced

2 large garlic cloves, minced

1 Bouquet Garni, 17

¼ teaspoon ground black pepper

¼ teaspoon ground mace (optional)

Reduce the heat and simmer until the chicken is well cooked, about 1 hour. Remove the chicken to a plate and let cool. Meanwhile, add to the soup pot:

2 medium Maine or new potatoes, diced

Simmer until tender, 15 to 20 minutes. Discard the bouquet garni and turn off the heat. When the chicken is cool enough to handle, remove and discard the skin and bones. Shred the meat and add to the soup. Reheat over medium heat and season with:

¼ cup chopped fresh parsley

Salt and ground black pepper to taste

Ladle into warmed bowls.

Vietnamese Beef Noodle Soup (Pho Bo)

About 12 cups; 4 to 6 servings

In Vietnam, this light, flavorful, visually exciting soup is a favorite for breakfast, lunch, and dinner. It has given rise to numerous pho restaurants all over the United States.

BEFORE COOKING:

Have ready:

¼ cup thinly sliced peeled fresh ginger

1 medium onion, sliced

3½ pounds oxtail, cut into 2-inch pieces (have your butcher do this)

One 3-inch cinnamon stick

6 star anise

1 tablespoon salt

1 teaspoon light or dark soy sauce

One 1-inch piece Chinese yellow rock sugar (optional)

Place on a plate:

12 ounces round steak, sliced as thinly as possible (more easily done if partially frozen)

Place on a second plate:

2 serrano peppers, thinly sliced

24 fresh basil leaves, halved

¼ cup 2-inch pieces scallion, halved lengthwise

Place on a third plate:

2 cups bean sprouts

3 tablespoons coarsely chopped fresh basil

Lime wedges

3 fresh chili peppers, coarsely chopped

TO COOK:

Heat a large soup pot over medium-high heat. When fairly hot, turn in the ginger and onion slices. Cook, stirring, until fragrant.

Add the oxtail and cook, stirring, briefly. Stir in:

3½ quarts cold water

Bring to a boil. Skim off the impurities that rise to the surface.

Stir in the cinnamon, star anise, salt, soy sauce, and rock sugar if using. Reduce the heat and simmer the soup for 2½ to 3 hours, skimming as needed. Strain and reserve.

About 30 minutes before the broth is done, soak in cold water to cover:

12 ounces dried flat rice stick noodles (banh pho)

Bring to a boil in a large pot:

4 quarts water

Add the rice stick noodles. Cook for about 1 minute. Drain.

TO SERVE:

Divide the noodles among individual soup bowls.

Add the slices of raw beef to each bowl, arranging them attractively. Divide the serrano peppers, basil leaves, and scallions among the bowls.

While arranging the individual soup bowls, bring the beef broth to a boil over high heat. Immediately fill each bowl with the boiling broth and serve. If the broth is added at the table, diners have the pleasure of watching it cook the beef and noodles.

Place the plate of bean sprouts, basil, lime, and chili peppers on the table, allowing diners to help themselves.

RICE STICK NOODLES

These thin, flat, translucent rice noodles should be soaked for 30 minutes in cold water, then boiled for 4 to 7 minutes before being added to any dish. They are most commonly used in pad thai and other stir-fried dishes and soups. Rice sticks are known as *banh pho* in Vietnam and *jantabon* in Thailand. Asian noodles are best understood by the type of flour or starch with which they are made. When looking for substitutes, choose noodles in the same starch family.

Oxtail Soup

About 5 cups

One story claims this rich meaty soup was born of necessity during the French Reign of Terror in 1793. Historically, hides were delivered to the tanneries complete with tails. These were commonly thrown away, until one day a hungry nobleman pleaded for a tail and made it into soup.

Heat in a soup pot over medium-high heat:

1½ tablespoons extra-virgin olive oil

Add and brown on all sides:

2 pounds oxtail (about 1 disjointed oxtail)

Stir in:

6 cups water
1 large carrot, peeled and diced
1 large celery stalk, diced

1 large onion, diced
2 cloves garlic, peeled
4 black peppercorns

Bring to a boil, reduce the heat, and simmer, partially covered, until the meat comes effortlessly from the bone, 3 to 4 hours. As the water evaporates during cooking, add only enough water to keep the meat submerged. Remove the oxtail from the soup. Discard the fat and bones and reserve the meat. Refrigerate the soup until cold, then remove the fat. When ready to serve, return the meat to the soup. Heat and season with:

¼ teaspoon salt

Ladle into warmed bowls. Garnish with:

Chopped fresh parsley

Pass at the table:

Ground black pepper

OXTAIL SOUP WITH VEGETABLES

The rich flavor of oxtail goes well with the tender vegetables in this soup. Prepare Oxtail Soup, left, adding with the salt: 1 medium leek (white part only), cut into thin strips; 1 small carrot, cut into thin strips; 1 small celery stalk, cut into thin strips; ¼ teaspoon additional salt. Simmer until the vegetables are tender, about 15 minutes. Add the meat and complete as directed.

French Simmered Beef and Vegetables (Pot-au-Feu)

About 10 cups broth; 4 to 6 servings

This hearty French boiled dinner features a variety of meats, mostly beef, and vegetables. The cooking broth is strained, seasoned, and served first in warmed bowls, then the meat and marrowbones are presented on a serving platter, accompanied by mustard and cornichons (French pickles), and toast on which to spread the succulent marrow.

Combine in a large soup pot, and cover with cold water:

4 beef short ribs (about 2½ pounds)
4 beef marrowbones, wrapped in cheesecloth
2 pounds beef shank, cut into 2-inch-thick slices

Bring to a boil, reduce the heat to low, and simmer, partially covered, for 2 hours. Stir in:

4 chicken thighs, skin removed
12 ounces whole sausage
4 medium carrots, cut into 1-inch pieces
4 medium leeks (white and tender green parts), cleaned thoroughly, halved lengthwise, and cut into 1-inch pieces
2 medium turnips, peeled and cut into 1-inch pieces
3 medium celery stalks, cut into 1-inch pieces

Simmer, partially covered, until the chicken is cooked, 30 to 40 minutes. Remove and reserve the meat and vegetables. Strain the broth and return it to the pot. Reduce to 10 cups over high heat. Slice the beef shank and sausage, then arrange the meat, vegetables, and marrowbones on a platter. Cover with aluminum foil and keep warm in a 200°F oven. Skim the fat off the surface of the broth with a ladle. Season with:

1½ teaspoons salt
Ground black pepper to taste

Heat the broth and ladle into warmed bowls. Serve the meat platter accompanied with:

Dijon or whole-grain mustard
Coarse salt
Cornichons
Toasted sliced French bread

Irish Stew

4 to 6 servings

The potatoes in this recipe are cut in two different ways because they serve different purposes. Those that are sliced break down during the long cooking and thicken the stew without the addition of flour. The halved potatoes cook to tender and add soft bite to the stew. As in a French blanquette, the meat is not browned.

Preheat the oven to 325°F.

Heat in a Dutch oven over medium heat:

2 tablespoons vegetable oil or unsalted butter

Add and cook without browning, until softened:

2 medium onions, chopped

Stir in:

3 pounds boneless lamb stew meat, cut into 1-inch cubes, or 3 pounds lamb shoulder chops

2 teaspoons fresh thyme leaves, or ¾ teaspoon dried

Salt and ground black pepper to taste

Mix in:

2 medium boiling potatoes, peeled and sliced

3 cups *Chicken Stock*, 22, or water

½ teaspoon Worcestershire sauce

Add:

4 medium potatoes, peeled and halved

Cover tightly and bake for 1 hour. Remove from the oven and add, stirring:

8 medium carrots, peeled and cut diagonally into ½-inch slices

¼ cup pearl barley

¼ cup heavy cream

Cover and return to the oven. Bake until the meat is fork-tender and barley is softened, 45 to 60 minutes more.

Season with:

Salt and ground black pepper to taste

Serve sprinkled with:

Chopped fresh parsley

Mulligatawny Soup

About 5 cups

The predecessors of this version were created by local cooks in southern India. The countless variations are all curried and then smoothed with coconut milk or cream.

Skin, bone, and cut into bite-sized pieces:

2 pounds chicken thighs

Heat over medium-high heat in a soup pot:

3 tablespoons vegetable oil

Add and cook, stirring, until golden brown, 7 to 8 minutes:

1 medium onion, thinly sliced

Add and cook, stirring, for 30 seconds:

2 cloves garlic, finely minced

One 1-inch piece fresh ginger, peeled and finely minced

1 tablespoon curry powder

Add the chicken along with:

2 tablespoons water

Cook, stirring, until the chicken loses its raw color and the oil sizzles and pools around the meat, 3 to 4 minutes. Stir in:

4 cups Chicken Stock, 22

½ teaspoon salt

Bring to a boil, reduce the heat to medium, and simmer until the chicken is cooked through, 20 to 30 minutes. Stir in:

1 cup unsweetened coconut milk (optional)

Simmer for 5 minutes more. Divide among 4 bowls:

½ cup hot cooked rice

Ladle the soup on top and garnish with:

Fresh coriander leaves

Lemon wedges

Chopped apples

Madras Curry Powder

About 1⅓ cups

Curry (or kari) leaves are the leaves of the kari plant, used to flavor the cooking of southern and southwestern India. Fresh leaves are sold at Indian specialty stores. You may substitute dried leaves, but their flavor is much less pungent.

Toast in a heated skillet over medium heat until a shade darker and fragrant, about 4 minutes:

6 tablespoons whole coriander seeds

4 tablespoons whole cumin seeds

3 tablespoons *chana dal* or yellow split peas

1 tablespoon black peppercorns

1 tablespoon black mustard seeds

5 dried red chili peppers

10 fresh or dried curry leaves (optional)

Combine the toasted spices with:

2 tablespoons fenugreek seeds

Grind the mixture to a powder in batches in a spice mill or electric coffee grinder. Mix well with:

3 tablespoons turmeric

Store in an airtight container in a cool place.

Barley Soup with Sausages (Minestra d'Orzo)

About 16 cups (4 quarts)

This soup is inspired by the foods of Italy's mountainous Tyrol at Austria's border. On its native turf, it would be flavored with "speck," meaty chunks of pork deeply smoked and cured with salt, juniper, garlic, and spices. Smoked kielbasa or bratwurst can be substituted. Serve with thick slices of country bread.

Cook in a medium skillet, or on a medium-hot outdoor or stovetop grill, until browned on all sides and heated through:

6 ounces deeply smoked sausages

Slice the sausages thinly and place in a large soup pot along with:

16 cups (4 quarts) *Vegetable Stock,* **20, or** *Chicken Stock,* **22**
1¼ cups pearl barley
2 large bay leaves, crumbled

Bring to a boil, reduce the heat, and simmer, partially covered, for 30 minutes. Meanwhile, heat in a large skillet over medium heat:

2 tablespoons extra-virgin olive oil

Add:

½ large head green cabbage, chopped

Cook, stirring, until the cabbage begins to color, 5 to 10 minutes. Add:

2 medium onions, finely chopped
1 large carrot, peeled and finely chopped
1 large celery stalk with leaves, finely chopped
3 tablespoons tightly packed fresh parsley leaves, minced
Two 3-inch sprigs fresh rosemary, or 2 teaspoons dried

Cook, stirring often, until the onions are browned, 10 to 15 minutes. Stir in:

3 tablespoons tightly packed fresh marjoram leaves, minced, or 1 tablespoon dried

1 large clove garlic, minced

Add 1 cup liquid from the soup pot and scrape the bottom of the skillet to loosen any browned bits. Stir the contents of the skillet into the soup pot along with:

2 red or white new potatoes, peeled and diced

Cover and simmer gently until the barley is tender but not mushy and the potatoes are cooked but firm, about 30 minutes more. If the soup is too thick, thin with water as needed. Season with:

2½ teaspoons salt
1 teaspoon ground black pepper

Ladle into warmed bowls. Sprinkle each serving with:

1 to 2 tablespoons shredded aged Montasio or imported provolone cheese

Beef Chili (Chili con Carne)

6 to 8 servings

For more flavor in this dish (opposite), make your own chili powder. As a rule of thumb, use smaller amounts of hotter peppers, such as arbol or serrano, and larger amounts of the mild and midrange varieties, such as ancho, mild New Mexico (red Anaheim), and guajillo. The steamed rice and sour cream help cool the heat of this dish. Bear in mind that any leftovers will become hotter from the heat of the chili powder and peppers the longer they are kept.

Toast in a skillet over medium heat for 1 to 2 minutes:

1 recipe *New Mexican Chili Powder*, right, or 1 cup store-bought chili powder

Set aside. Pat dry:

3 pounds beef chuck, trimmed and cut into ½-inch cubes

Season with:

1 to 2 teaspoons salt

Heat in a cast-iron skillet over medium-high heat:

1 tablespoon olive oil

Brown the meat in batches, adding more oil if needed. Remove the browned meat to a Dutch oven.

Add to the cast-iron skillet:

1 tablespoon olive oil
2 large onions, minced
10 cloves garlic, minced
7 fresh jalapeño peppers, stemmed, seeded, and minced
½ teaspoon salt

Cook, stirring often, over medium-high heat until the vegetables are softened, 6 to 8 minutes. Remove to the Dutch oven with the meat. Stir the toasted spices into the meat mixture and cook for 2 minutes over medium-high heat. Add:

One 28-ounce can plum tomatoes, with juice
1 tablespoon red wine vinegar
6 cups water

Season with:

Salt to taste

Simmer, uncovered, until the meat is tender and the sauce is reduced and thickened, about 1½ hours.

Serve with:

Hot cooked rice
Sour cream

New Mexican Chili Powder

About ½ cup

Based on ground dried chilies, this chili powder is a blend created to flavor Southwestern dishes. It is as individual as the person who prepares it. Sometimes it is very dark, sometimes a rusty red. This chili powder is best toasted before use. Stir it in a medium skillet over the lowest heat until you can smell the spices.

Combine in a small bowl:

5 tablespoons ground mild chili peppers, such as New Mexico, pasilla, or ancho
2 tablespoons dried oregano
1½ tablespoons ground cumin
½ teaspoon ground red pepper, or to taste

Ohio Farmhouse Sausage Chili

4 to 6 servings

A delicious "warmer-upper" after a fine tramp in the woods on a chilly day. Loose pork sausage meat is used instead of ground beef. Look for some that is not heavily spiced. Corn bread is perfect served alongside.

Brown in a large skillet:

1 pound pork sausage
1 large onion, chopped

Toward the end of the browning, add:

1 celery stalk, diced

When the celery is softened, add:

One 28-ounce can (3½ cups) whole tomatoes, chopped
2 cups tomato juice or *Chicken Broth*, 29, or a mixture of the two
1 to 2 tablespoons maple syrup or molasses
2 teaspoons ground cumin
1½ teaspoons powdered sage
½ teaspoon ground black pepper

Simmer for 20 minutes. Add:

3½ to 4 cups cooked red kidney beans, drained and rinsed

Simmer for 15 minutes more.

Serve with:

Sharp Cheddar cheese, cubed
***Northern Corn Bread*, 124**

Brunswick Stew

6 to 8 servings

This Southern specialty is commonly served as a side dish with barbecue but can easily stand on its own as a main course. Chicken, lima beans, and corn are the main ingredients, with such meats as rabbit, pork, or even squirrel sometimes added to the pot as well. This version includes barbecue sauce, which makes it especially rich and thick.

Rinse and pat dry:

5 pounds chicken parts

Season with:

**Salt and ground black pepper
  to taste**

**½ teaspoon ground red pepper
  (optional)**

Heat in a large, heavy Dutch oven over medium-high heat until shimmery:

**2 tablespoons bacon fat or
  vegetable oil**

Add the chicken pieces in small batches and brown on all sides; remove them to a plate as they are done. Remove all but 2 tablespoons of the fat in the pan. Reduce the heat to medium and add:

1 cup chopped onions

1 cup chopped celery

Cook, stirring occasionally, until the vegetables are just tender, 5 to 7 minutes. Return the chicken with the accumulated juices to the pan. Add:

3 cups lima beans, fresh or frozen

**2 cups barbecued pork or
  smoked ham, cut into ½-inch
  chunks (optional)**

**1½ to 2 cups chopped seeded
  peeled tomatoes, fresh or
  canned**

1 cup barbecue sauce

1 cup tomato puree

1 cup *Chicken Stock*, 22, or water

**1 tablespoon minced garlic
  (optional)**

2 bay leaves

**Salt and ground black pepper
  to taste**

Ground red pepper to taste

Bring the stew to a boil over high heat. Reduce the heat to low, cover the pan, and simmer gently until the chicken is nearly tender, 35 to 45 minutes. Add:

3 cups corn kernels, fresh or frozen

Simmer, uncovered, for 10 minutes more. Skim any fat from the gravy with a spoon. Season the stew to taste with:

Salt and ground black pepper

**Several drops of Worcestershire
  sauce**

**Several drops of hot red pepper
  sauce**

If you wish, sprinkle the top with:

Minced fresh parsley

Fresh breadcrumbs, toasted

MAKING BREADCRUMBS

Place slices of good, stale bread on a baking sheet in a 200°F oven for 1 to 2 hours; do not let them brown. Grind the dry bread into crumbs with the grating blade of a food processor or a hand grater. Spread on a baking sheet in a 375°F oven for 10 to 15 minutes. For seasoned breadcrumbs, add ½ teaspoon salt to every 1 cup dry breadcrumbs; melt ⅓ cup butter per 1 cup crumbs in a skillet and toss the crumbs in the butter until browned. Spices, herbs, or grated hard cheese can be added while toasting the bread-crumbs. Cook until the butter is absorbed and the crumbs are golden brown.

MacLeid's Rockcastle Chili

8 to 10 servings

This is camp chef extraordinaire and good friend Matt MacLeid's Saturday-night staple on our camping trips to the Rockcastle River Gorge.

Sauté in a large skillet until cracklings are golden brown:

½ pound bacon, diced

Remove the bacon using a slotted spoon. In the drippings, sauté briefly:

1½ pounds round steak, coarsely ground or chopped in a food processor

6 to 12 large cloves garlic, coarsely chopped

2 large onions, coarsely chopped

Deglaze the skillet until foam disappears, with:

One 12-ounce bottle dark beer

Remove all to a large pot or Dutch oven. Stir in:

One 32-ounce can tomatoes, with juice

One 16-ounce can kidney beans, with juice

One 16-ounce can great Northern beans, with juice

One 16-ounce can pinto beans, with juice

6 tablespoons ancho chili powder

2 tablespoons ground cumin

1 tablespoon ground black pepper

1½ cups water or one 12-ounce bottle dark beer

Simmer for about 3 hours, covered, stirring occasionally to prevent sticking. Season to taste with:

Salt and ground black pepper

Red pepper sauce

Serve with:

Southern Corn Bread, 123

Diced sharp Cheddar cheese

GRINDING MEAT

Now that the food processor is a fundamental tool in most kitchens, it is very easy to grind your own meat. By chopping your own meat, you have a better guarantee of freshness and fat content. The best cuts to use are chuck or shoulder. Trim away visible fat and cut the meat into 1-inch cubes. Keep the meat thoroughly refrigerated before and after chopping. Place enough meat in the bowl of the processor to cover the blade by 1 inch, no more. Pulse the processor until the pieces of meat are uniformly small (about ⅛ inch). Remove the chopped meat from the bowl and repeat the process until all the meat is done.

Cincinnati Chili Cockaigne

6 servings

There are hundreds of so-called original recipes for John Kiradjieff's Cincinnati Chili that he served for the first time in Cincinnati's first chili parlor, The Empress. We particularly like this version of our hometown obsession, and we can guarantee without question that it is not the one of myth.

In a 4- to 6-quart pot, bring to a boil:

1 quart water

Add:

2 pounds ground chuck

Stir until separated and reduce heat to a simmer. Add:

2 medium onions, finely chopped

5 to 6 cloves garlic, crushed

One 15-ounce can tomato sauce

2 tablespoons cider vinegar

1 tablespoon Worcestershire sauce

Stir and add:

10 peppercorns, ground

8 whole allspice, ground

8 whole cloves, ground

1 large bay leaf

2 teaspoons salt

2 teaspoons ground cinnamon

1½ teaspoons ground red pepper

1 teaspoon ground cumin

½ ounce unsweetened chocolate, grated

Return to a boil, then reduce the heat to a simmer, for 2½ hours cooking time in all. Cool uncovered and refrigerate overnight. Before serving, skim off all or most of the fat and discard. Reheat the chili for a 2-Way, and serve over:

Cooked spaghetti

For a 3-Way, add:

Grated Cheddar cheese

For a 4-Way, sprinkle on:

Chopped onions

For a 5-Way, top each serving with:

¼ cup cooked red kidney beans

Traditional sides also include:

Oyster crackers

Hot red pepper sauce

ABOUT **FRUIT** SOUPS

We include recipes for fruit soups that are traditionally served as first courses. Feel free to present them as desserts, however. Whichever place they occupy on your menu, they are easy to make, and they cleanse the palate. For fresh fruit, the best advice is to eat fruit that is local, in season, and perfectly ripe.

Melon Soup, 115

Cherry Soup

About 6 cups

We make this fruit soup in the summer with fresh cherries and serve it cold before the main course. In the winter, we use canned or bottled cherries and serve it heated.

Have ready:

2 pounds cherries, stemmed and pitted, or 4 cups stemmed and pitted canned cherries, drained

Place half of the cherries in a soup pot, along with:

2 cups water

2 cups Gewürztraminer or medium-dry white wine

Bring to a boil, reduce the heat, and simmer until the cherries are soft, about 15 minutes. Puree until smooth. Stir together in a small bowl:

¼ cup sugar

4 teaspoons cornstarch

Add 3 tablespoons of the cherry mixture to the cornstarch and sugar and stir well. Return the cherry puree and the cherry paste to the pot and cook over high heat, whisking until thickened, about 5 minutes. Reduce the heat and stir in the reserved cherries along with:

1 tablespoon fresh orange juice

1 tablespoon fresh lemon juice

1 teaspoon grated orange zest

Simmer until warmed through. Taste for sweetness; if not sweet enough, add additional:

Sugar

If too sweet, add additional:

Lemon juice

Serve warm or cold, garnished with:

Dollop of sour cream or yogurt

Fresh mint sprigs

CHERRIES

Pitted raw sweet cherries are incomparable in cold soups. Bings are the favorite of commercial growers because they grow easily, taste good, and travel well. Fresh light-skinned Royal Anns and Rainiers are more fragile than Bings and are seen outside of cherry country only for short periods. Sweet cherries are available late May through July; August fruits are from cold storage or of inferior quality.

Sour cherries, another variety, are tastier after cooking, since they are very acid and heat helps them absorb sweetening. Although most commercial sour cherries are canned, you may find fresh morellos, delightful with their red juice, or amarelles, with their clear juice, close to where they are grown. Sour cherries ripen a couple of weeks after sweet cherries. Montmorency, a morello, is the principal sour cherry in this country. It is predominantly grown in New England,

around the Great Lakes, and on the Great Plains. Heart-shaped Duke cherries are a sweet-and-sour cross.

All cherries are sent to market ripe. Choose them individually (never prepackaged) after tasting one for flavor. Select the largest, glossiest, plumpest, and firmest with the greenest stems. For sweet cherries, choose the darkest; for sour cherries, the brightest. Avoid stemless cherries—the wound is an invitation to bacteria, as evidenced when there is brown around the stem scar. If there are soft or spoiling cherries in a bin, do not buy any. The taste of mold can permeate surrounding fruit.

To prepare cherries, rinse and stem them (**1**). Pit them with a cherry pitter by pushing the plunger of the cherry pitter through the stem scar, pitting one by one into a small empty bowl (**2**).

Melon Soup

About 8 cups

Ripe cantaloupe and freshly squeezed juices are essential to this soup.
Puree in a food processor until smooth:

2 medium very ripe and sweet cantaloupes or other orange-fleshed melons, peeled, seeded, and cut into chunks

Pour into a large bowl and stir in:

1 cup fresh orange juice
¼ cup fresh lime juice
2 tablespoons fresh lemon juice

Refrigerate until cold, about 2 hours. When ready to serve, prepare:

¼ cup freshly grated peeled ginger

Using a cheesecloth or your hands, squeeze out the ginger juice into a small bowl. Stir 4 teaspoons of the juice into the soup. Serve in chilled bowls, garnished with:

Thinly sliced kiwi fruit or strawberries
Fresh mint sprigs

Fruit Soup

About 6 cups

In many Scandinavian homes in the Midwest, this soup is set out on the buffet table. It is good hot or cold.
Combine in a large saucepan and let stand for 45 minutes:

¾ cup dried apricots or peaches, quartered
¾ cup dried prunes, pitted and quartered
3 tablespoons raisins
2 tablespoons dried currants

Two 3-inch cinnamon sticks
Grated zest of 1 orange
3 tablespoons quick-cooking tapioca
4 cups apple juice, cranberry juice, or water

Stir in:

Up to ¼ cup of sugar

Bring to a boil, reduce the heat to low, and simmer, stirring occasionally, until the fruit is softened and the soup is thickened, about 30 minutes. Stir in:

2 red apples, peeled, cored, and cut into 1-inch pieces

Cook until the apples are tender, about 8 minutes. Let cool and remove the cinnamon sticks. Serve warm or cold, garnished with:

Crème fraîche, sour cream, or heavy cream

DRIED FRUITS

The high caloric and nutritive values of dried fruits can be readily grasped if you consider that it takes 5½ pounds fresh apricots to yield 1 pound dried. The fruits are suddenly not so expensive when you realize that there is no waste except the pits and that you are getting concentrated food value. When selecting dried fruits, look for the biggest and brightest, the plumpest, and those with uniform color. Avoid fruits with blemishes and packages containing pieces of stalks or damaged fruits. Check for unnecessary additives. When a new box or package is opened, do not store the fruits in the opened container. Dried fruits should be stored in tightly covered glass containers in a cool (45° to 50°F), dark, dry place or the refrigerator. Glass is good because you can see if any moisture is collecting inside—moisture will cause dry foods to spoil. All varieties must be watched for insects. Store far from foods like onions and garlic, because the fruits readily absorb other odors. Should sugaring develop—crystals of sugar forming on the surface of the skin—you can dip the fruit in boiling water, drain, and dry at once. A cool, dry atmosphere will keep it from happening.

ABOUT
CONDIMENTS
& QUICK BREADS

*W*hereas condiments differ widely in what they contain and how they are used, each occupies the same location in the culinary firmament, somewhere between a single spice and a side dish to be eaten on its own. Condiments can spice up, cool down, or add richness to soups and stews. Every cook should have a few good recipes for salsas, sauces, and flavored mayonnaises in their repertoire. Bringing them to table can make an ordinary soup or stew special.

Quick breads are easy to make and a busy person's "rabbit from a hat." Homemade hot biscuits, for instance, can transform the simplest soup or stew into a satisfying meal.

Clockwise from top: *Basic Rolled Biscuits, 122; Salsa Fresca, 118; Pistou, 120*

Condiments for Soups and Stews

The characteristics of condiments tend to shift over time, but they do share a few attributes. All are used to provide flavor for food; all contain more than a single ingredient; all can be made in advance and most can be stored for at least a day or two, often much longer; and all stand alone, created independently and therefore able to add their distinctive flavors to a range of differ-

ent dishes. (This last characteristic distinguishes them from pan sauces, which draw much of their flavor from the browned bits left in the pan after cooking poultry or meat.)

Condiments possess qualities that make them particularly useful for today's cooks. Most of them are quick and easy to prepare, and their intense flavors can make even a plain soup or stew an interesting meal.

Also, since the recipes for condiments are flexible, a cook can adjust the flavor by adding more or less garlic, chili pepper, vinegar, spices, lime juice, and so on, depending on personal preference and on what the condiment will accompany.

Serve these condiments as a garnish for soups or stews, or put them out on the table so your guests can help themselves.

Salsa Fresca

About 2 cups

This recipe for Mexican salsa is easily doubled or tripled, but make only as much as you will use immediately, as it loses its texture on standing and the chili peppers increase in heat. Regional variations of salsa fresca include using scallions or white or red onions, water instead of lime juice, and in Yucatán, sour-orange juice instead of lime juice. Precise amounts are less important than the happy marriage of flavors, so taste as you go.

Combine in a medium bowl:
½ small white or red onion or 8 slender scallions, finely chopped, rinsed, and drained
2 tablespoons fresh lime juice or cold water
Prepare the following ingredients, setting them aside, then add all together to the onion mixture:
2 large ripe tomatoes, or 3 to 5 ripe plum tomatoes, seeded, if desired, and finely diced

¼ to ½ cup chopped fresh cilantro (leaves and tender stems)
3 to 5 serrano or fresh jalapeño peppers, or ¼ to 1 habanero pepper, or to taste, seeded and minced
6 radishes, finely diced (optional)
1 medium clove garlic, minced (optional)
Stir together well. Season with:
¼ teaspoon salt, or to taste
Serve immediately.

Garlic Mayonnaise (Aïoli)

About 1 cup

Sometimes called beurre de Provence—*the butter of Provence— aïoli is traditionally served slightly chilled as a sauce for cold poached fish, vegetables, meat, or eggs. It also makes a luxurious garnish for hot and cold soups. Aïoli is a contraction of the Provençal words for garlic and oil.* Whisk together in a medium bowl until smooth and light:

2 large egg yolks
4 to 6 cloves garlic, finely minced
Salt and ground white pepper to taste
Whisk in by drops until the mixture starts to thicken and stiffen:
1 cup olive oil, or part olive and part safflower or peanut oil, at room temperature
As the sauce begins to thicken,

whisk in the oil more steadily, making sure each addition is thoroughly blended before adding the next. Gradually whisk in:
1 teaspoon fresh lemon juice, or to taste
½ teaspoon cold water
Taste and adjust the seasonings. Serve immediately or refrigerate in a jar for 1 to 2 days.

Roasted Tomato-Jalapeño Salsa

About 2 cups

Heat the broiler. Arrange on a rimmed baking sheet:

1 pound red, ripe tomatoes

Broil 4 inches from the heat until they blister, darken, and soften on one side, about 4 minutes; turn them over and broil the other side until blistered and darkened, 5 to 6 minutes. Meanwhile, heat a dry cast-iron griddle or skillet over high heat, and add:

2 large fresh jalapeño peppers
3 cloves garlic, unpeeled

Shake them in the pan until their skins are soft and charred here and there, 5 to 10 minutes for the jalapeños, about 15 minutes for the garlic. Let cool, then peel the tomatoes, reserving the juices, pull the stems off the jalapeños, and peel the garlic.

Place the jalapeños and garlic in a food processor or blender with:

¼ teaspoon salt

Process to a coarse paste. Add the tomatoes and process a few times until you have a coarse-textured puree. Stir in:

½ small white onion, finely
**   chopped, rinsed, and drained**
Generous ⅓ cup loosely packed
**   chopped fresh cilantro**
About 1½ teaspoons cider
**   vinegar (optional)**

Add 2 to 4 tablespoons water, if necessary, to give the salsa a fairly thick but easily spoonable consistency. Taste and season with:

Salt

Serve immediately.

JALAPEÑO PEPPER

These stubby green to red chilies are widely available and can vary considerably in their heat from totally mild (a new heatless jalapeño is now being grown for use in commercial American salsa) to quite hot varieties found in farmers' markets and their homeland of Veracruz, Mexico. The jalapeño pepper's bright green, juicy, grassy taste works well in many dishes, from raw salsas to soups and stews. This pepper is also good stuffed and fried. When mature jalapeños are smoked and dried, they are known as chipotles. Fresh jalapeños measure about 2½ inches in length and ¾ inch wide at the stem end and taper a little before coming to a rather blunt tip.

Saffron Garlic Mayonnaise (Rouille)

About 1 cup

This thick, garlicky, bright-gold sauce is the essential finish for Bouillabaisse, 86, and other Provençal fish soups and stews. It is also wonderful with fish, seafood, meats, poultry, and vegetables from the oven or grill. All rouilles are brilliant in color. Some cooks use pureed roasted red peppers, but we vote for saffron.

Stir together in a small bowl, cover, and let stand for 10 minutes:

¾ teaspoon saffron threads, or
**   ⅛ teaspoon powdered saffron**
2 tablespoons hot stock from the
**   soup to be garnished, or water**

Process in a food processor to fine crumbs:

1 fresh French roll (not sour-
**   dough), crust trimmed**

Add ¾ cup of the breadcrumbs to the saffron infusion. Mash with a fork to a loose paste, stirring in, if necessary:

Up to 1 tablespoon hot stock
**   or water**

Place in a mortar or small bowl:

1 large dried red chili pepper,
**   seeded**

Vigorously pound to a powder with a pestle or sturdy wooden spoon. Add and pound until the garlic is pureed:

3 small cloves garlic, peeled
⅛ teaspoon coarse salt

Stir in:

1 large egg yolk

Stir in the bread paste bit by bit, then

work vigorously until blended and smooth. Whisk in by drops until the mixture starts to thicken and stiffen:

About ¾ cup olive oil, or part
**   olive and part safflower oil,**
**   at room temperature**

Let the oil fall to one side of the mortar or bowl, very slowly at first, while you stir it in without stopping. (If the sauce should start to curdle, simply stir in a little hot stock or water.) When the mixture has absorbed all the oil it can, season with:

Salt to taste

Cover and refrigerate. Use the same day.

Pistou

About 1 cup

The Provençal version of Italy's pesto, made without nuts, makes a great addition to soups and stews.

Vigorously pound to a paste with a mortar and pestle, or process in a food processor or blender until the garlic is minced:

4 to 6 large cloves garlic, peeled
Pinch of coarse salt

Gradually add and pound, or process, to a dark green paste:

2 cups packed fresh basil leaves

Add in 4 batches and pound, or pulse, to the consistency of soft butter:

½ cup grated Parmesan or Gruyère cheese

Gradually add and pound, or with the machine running, pour through the feed tube in a slow, steady stream, until the sauce has the consistency of coarse mayonnaise:

⅓ cup olive oil, preferably extra virgin

Season with:

Salt and ground black pepper to taste

Serve at room temperature or store, covered and refrigerated, for up to 2 days.

Avgolemono

About 1¼ cups

This favorite Greek sauce is good with soups and stews—anything, say the Greeks, that is not made with garlic or tomatoes.

Stir together in a small bowl:

1 tablespoon cold water
1 teaspoon cornstarch

Whisk together in a small, heavy stainless-steel saucepan over low heat just until warm:

3 large egg yolks
3 to 4 tablespoons fresh lemon juice

Pour the cornstarch mixture into the egg mixture. Gradually add, stirring or whisking constantly:

1 cup *Vegetable Stock*, 20, or *Express Chicken Broth*, 29

Cook, stirring constantly, over medium-low heat until thick and creamy and the sauce coats the back of a spoon; do not let the sauce get too hot, or the eggs will curdle. Remove the sauce from the heat and stir in:

Salt and ground black pepper to taste

Serve immediately.

Nam Prik (Thai Hot Sauce)

About ⅔ cup

Nam prik, which translates as "pepper water," is the traditional table sauce of Thailand. It is stirred into soups, as well as used to season rice, noodles, or vegetables. The sauce is best a day or two after making, and keeps well in the refrigerator. If dried shrimp and fish sauce are not available, add more fresh or dried chili peppers and lime juice.

Pound to a paste with a mortar and pestle or process in a small food processor or blender:

18 tiny dried shrimp, chopped
4 small dried red chili peppers, seeded, if desired, and crumbled
4 cloves garlic, chopped
2 tablespoons fresh lime juice
1 tablespoon fish sauce

Stir in:

3 small red or green serrano peppers, seeded, if desired, and finely chopped
Chopped fresh cilantro to taste
A little brown sugar (optional)
Cover and refrigerate for at least 1 day before serving.

Chili Oil

About ¾ cup

This oil is exceedingly hot—use sparingly. A few drops are superb in Asian soups. Although there are many different peppers in Asian markets labeled "Thai peppers," perhaps the most common in this country are the small, elongated, pointy green to red peppers sold with their stems attached. These intensely hot peppers measure about

1 ½ inches long and only ¼ inch wide. Other names are bird and bird's-eye.
Coarsely chop in a blender or spice grinder:
1 cup dried chili peppers, preferably Thai
Transfer to a stainless-steel saucepan and add:
¾ cup peanut oil

Cook over medium heat until the peppers begin to foam. Remove from the heat when some of the smallest flecks on the side of the pan blacken. Cover, and let sit for 4 to 6 hours. Strain through a dampened paper coffee filter into a scrupulously clean jar or bottle. This keeps, covered and refrigerated, for up to 1 month.

Harissa

About ⅓ cup

In North Africa, this fiery pepper paste is stirred into soups and seafood stews.
Combine in a small dry skillet over medium heat and toast, shaking the pan often to prevent burning, until very aromatic, 2 to 3 minutes:
1 teaspoon caraway seeds
1 teaspoon coriander seeds
½ teaspoon cumin seeds
Remove from the heat, let cool to room temperature, and grind to a fine powder in a spice grinder, coffee grinder, blender, or with a mortar and pestle. Add and grind again until smooth:

2 cloves garlic, quartered
Salt to taste
Add and grind until all the ingredients are well combined:
3 tablespoons sweet paprika
1 tablespoon red pepper flakes
1 tablespoon olive oil
The harissa will be very thick and dry. Transfer the paste to a small jar and cover with:
Olive oil
Store, covered, in the refrigerator; it will keep for 6 months.

PAPRIKA

Finely ground dried ripe peppers constitute this spice. Depending on the pepper used, the color varies from light orange to deep red, the flavor from bland to rich but mild. *Sweet* paprika is ground from the flesh of particularly sweet peppers with most, if not all, of their seeds and ribs removed—these parts can be sharp tasting. The best paprika has long come from Hungary, where paprika making is an important culinary tradition.

Breads for Serving with Soups and Stews

Quick breads are so called because they are quickly mixed and, with the absence of yeast, need no lengthy rising time before baking. Thus gratification is never delayed. These breads encompass biscuits, corn breads, and savory loaves to serve with soups and stews.

Biscuits are commonly served alongside stews. A survey of good biscuit recipes proves that they are quite forgiving. Some cooks use twice the amount of baking powder. Some use four times the amount of butter.

Even the size of the fat pieces cut into the flour varies. Nor is there a precise proportion of liquid to flour, for good rolled biscuits seem to be made from both fairly stiff and soft doughs. For novice cooks, it is worth noting that the easiest biscuit of all to make is the drop biscuit, which requires no rolling or cutting—and less cleanup afterward.

Corn bread, a hearty quick bread made with coarse meal, is well suited to serving with soups and stews. Anyone who grew up on southern corn bread knows the hankering for its rich brown crust, crunchy edges, and slightly gritty bite. The ultimate southern experience demands both stone-ground meal *and* a preheated heavy pan to supply the required crustiness. The cakier northern corn bread also reaches its pinnacle with stone-ground meal.

Like corn bread, other savory quick breads are made from simple batters that can be studded with all kinds of ingredients—from olives and nuts to bacon and cheese.

Basic Rolled Biscuits

Twenty 2-inch biscuits

You can shape and cut essentially any shape you like with this dough. These biscuits go nicely alongside a hearty stew or flavorful soup.

Position a rack in the center of the oven. Preheat the oven to 450°F. Have ready a large ungreased baking sheet.

Whisk together thoroughly in a large bowl:

2 cups all-purpose flour
2½ teaspoons baking powder
½ to ¾ teaspoon salt

Drop in:

5 to 6 tablespoons cold unsalted butter, cut into pieces

Cut in the butter with 2 knives or a pastry blender, tossing the pieces with the flour mixture to coat and separate them as you work. For biscuits with crunchy edges and a flaky, layered structure, continue to cut in the butter until the largest pieces are the size of peas and the rest resemble breadcrumbs. For classic fluffy biscuits, continue to cut in the butter until the mixture resembles coarse breadcrumbs. Do not allow the butter to melt or form a paste with the flour.

Add all at once:

¾ cup milk

Mix with a rubber spatula, wooden spoon, or fork just until most of the dry ingredients are moistened. With a lightly floured hand, gather the dough into a ball and knead it gently against the sides and bottom of the bowl 5 to 10 times, turning and pressing any loose pieces into the dough each time until they adhere and the bowl is fairly clean.

To shape round biscuits: Transfer the dough to a lightly floured surface. With a lightly floured rolling pin or your fingers, roll out or pat the dough ½ inch thick. Cut out 1¾- to 2-inch rounds with a drinking glass or biscuit cutter dipped in flour; push the cutter straight down into the dough and pull it out without twisting for biscuits that will rise evenly. You can reroll the scraps and cut additional biscuits (they are never as tender as the first-cut).

To shape square biscuits (with virtually no scraps): Roll out the dough ½ inch thick (¼ to ⅜ inch if cooking on a griddle) into a square or rectangle. Trim a fraction of an inch from the edges of the dough with a sharp knife before cutting into 2-inch squares.

For browner tops, you can brush the biscuit tops with:

Milk or melted butter

Place the biscuits on a baking sheet at least 1 inch apart for biscuits with crusty sides or close together for biscuits that are joined and remain soft on the sides. Bake until the biscuits are golden brown on the top and a deeper golden brown on the bottom, 10 to 12 minutes. Serve hot.

Cream Biscuits

Twenty 2-inch biscuits

Position a rack in the center of the oven. Preheat the oven to 450°F. Have ready a large ungreased baking sheet.
Whisk together thoroughly in a large bowl:

2 cups all-purpose flour
2½ teaspoons baking powder
½ to ¾ teaspoon salt

Add all at once:

1¼ cups heavy cream

Mix with a rubber spatula, wooden spoon, or fork just until most of the dry ingredients are moistened. Knead, shape, and bake as directed for *Basic Rolled Biscuits, opposite.* Serve hot.

Southern Corn Bread

8 servings

Real southern corn bread is made only with stone-ground cornmeal (tradition dictates white), buttermilk, eggs, leavening, and salt—no flour and no sugar. Some southern cooks stir in a tablespoon of bacon fat. The bread is moist and crusty.

Position a rack in the upper third of the oven. Preheat the oven to 450°F. Place in a heavy 9-inch skillet, preferably cast-iron, or less desirably, an 8 x 8-inch glass baking pan:

1 tablespoon bacon fat, lard, or
**   vegetable shortening**

Whisk together thoroughly in a large bowl:

1¾ cups stone-ground cornmeal,
**   preferably white**
1 tablespoon sugar (optional)
1 teaspoon baking powder
1 teaspoon baking soda
1 teaspoon salt (¾ teaspoon if
**   using buttermilk with salt)**

Whisk until foamy in another bowl:

2 large eggs

Whisk in:

2 cups buttermilk

Add the wet ingredients to the dry ingredients and whisk just until blended. Place the skillet or pan in

the oven and heat until the fat smokes. Pour in the batter all at once. Bake until the top is browned and the center feels firm when pressed, 20 to 25 minutes. Serve immediately from the pan, cut in wedges or squares, with:

Butter

Leftovers, though dry, are nice enough if wrapped in foil and rewarmed in a low oven.

CORN STICKS

Quick breads can be baked in any size pan with small adjustments to baking time. Use a corn stick pan for these favorites.

Prepare Southern Corn Bread, left. Generously brush a corn stick pan with oil or melted shortening and heat in a preheated 450°F oven until the fat smokes. Fill the cups two-thirds full. Bake for 10 to 15 minutes. Pry out onto a rack with a knife or fork. Brush out any crumbs, regrease, and continue with the rest of the batter. The yield will vary depending on the pan you use.

Northern Corn Bread

10 to 12 servings

Here a mixture of cornmeal and flour and a combination of milk and butter-milk yield a lighter corn bread with a more cakey texture than Southern Corn Bread, 123.

Position a rack in the center of the oven. Preheat the oven to 425°F. Grease a 9 x 9-inch pan or a standard 12-muffin pan or line the muffin pan with paper cups. Whisk together thoroughly in a large bowl:

1¼ cups stone-ground cornmeal
¾ cup all-purpose flour
1 to 4 tablespoons sugar
2 teaspoons baking powder
½ teaspoon baking soda
½ teaspoon salt

Whisk together in another bowl:

2 large eggs
⅔ cup milk
⅔ cup buttermilk

Add the wet ingredients to the dry ingredients and stir just until moistened. Fold in:

2 to 3 tablespoons warm melted unsalted butter or vegetable oil

Scrape the batter into the pan and tilt (if using a square pan) to spread evenly. Bake until a toothpick inserted in the center comes out clean, 10 to 12 minutes in a muffin pan, 20 to 25 minutes in a square pan. Serve hot.

Smoky Bacon, Cheese, and Roasted Hot Pepper Corn Bread

Very spicy, robust, and satisfying—possibly the best hot and spicy corn bread of them all.

Prepare and let cool:

2 fresh jalapeño peppers, roasted until the skins are blackened, skinned, seeded, and diced
1 red bell pepper, roasted until the skin is blackened, skinned, seeded, and diced
6 slices bacon, diced, fried until crisp, drained, and blotted

Combine in a medium bowl and toss with:

¾ cup shredded sharp Cheddar cheese

Prepare *Southern Corn Bread*, 123, using 1 tablespoon sugar and adding to the dry ingredients:

1 tablespoon chili powder

Fold the prepared pepper mixture into the completed batter.

MAKING CROUTONS

These dried or fried seasoned fresh bread morsels come in all sizes and are perfect for garnishing soups and stews. Croutons are made by cutting bread, preferably simple French bread, into small or large dice or square slices, buttering them or rubbing them with olive oil, and toasting in a 375°F oven until crisp, 10 to 15 minutes.

Mediterranean Olive Bread

8 to 10 servings

Position a rack in the lower third of the oven. Preheat the oven to 350°F. Grease an 8½ x 4½-inch (6-cup) loaf pan. Whisk together thoroughly:

1½ cups all-purpose flour
¾ cup whole-wheat flour
2½ teaspoons baking powder
¾ teaspoon dried rosemary, or 1 teaspoon chopped fresh
½ teaspoon salt

Whisk together in a large bowl:

2 large eggs
1 cup milk
¼ cup olive oil

Add the flour mixture and fold until about three-quarters of the dry ingredients are moistened. Add:

⅓ cup finely chopped walnuts
⅓ cup chopped pitted imported olives

Fold just until the pieces are distributed and the dry ingredients are moistened; the batter will be stiff. Scrape the batter into the pan and spread evenly. Bake until a toothpick inserted in the center comes out clean, 40 to 45 minutes. Let cool in the pan on a rack for 5 to 10 minutes before unmolding to cool completely on the rack.

Quick Beer Bread

8 servings

Serve with hearty soups or stews and cheeses. Slices are good toasted, or you can rewarm the whole loaf in the oven.
Position a rack in the lower third of the oven. Preheat the oven to 400°F. Grease an 8½ x 4½-inch (6-cup) loaf pan.
Whisk together thoroughly in a large bowl:

1 cup whole-wheat flour
1 cup all-purpose flour
½ cup old-fashioned rolled oats
2 tablespoons sugar
2 teaspoons baking powder
½ teaspoon baking soda
½ teaspoon salt
Add:
1½ cups light or dark beer (but not stout), cold or at room temperature but not flat

Fold just until the dry ingredients are moistened. Scrape the batter into the pan and spread evenly. Bake until a toothpick inserted in the center and all the way to the bottom of the pan comes out clean, 35 to 40 minutes. Let cool in the pan on a rack for 5 to 10 minutes before unmolding to cool completely on the rack.

Zucchini Cheddar Bread

10 to 12 servings

We make this whether or not the garden runneth over! Serve with soup for lunch or with a hearty stew for dinner. This is lovely toasted the next day.
Position a rack in the center of the oven. Preheat the oven to 350°F. Grease a 9 x 5-inch (8-cup) loaf pan.
Whisk together thoroughly in a large bowl:

3 cups all-purpose flour
4 teaspoons baking powder
1 teaspoon salt
½ teaspoon baking soda
Add and toss to separate and coat with flour:
1 cup coarsely shredded zucchini
¾ cup shredded sharp Cheddar cheese
¼ cup chopped scallions
3 tablespoons chopped fresh parsley
1 tablespoon snipped fresh dill, or 2 teaspoons dried
Whisk together in another bowl:
2 large eggs
1 cup buttermilk

4 tablespoons (½ stick) warm melted unsalted butter or vegetable oil
Add to the flour mixture and mix with a few light strokes just until the dry ingredients are moistened. Do not overmix; the batter should not be smooth. Bake until a toothpick inserted in the center comes out clean, 55 to 60 minutes. Let cool in the pan on a rack for 5 to 10 minutes before unmolding to cool completely on the rack.

ZUCCHINI

Zucchini, perhaps the best known summer squash, are thin, dark green, and 6 to 8 inches long. Select the smallest, firmest, glossiest squash, heaviest for their size, without soft spots or other blemishes. Store in perforated plastic vegetable bags in the refrigerator crisper. With their mild, sweet flesh, zucchini are excellent with most of summer's harvest, especially tomatoes, onions, peppers (both sweet and chili), garlic, oregano, marjoram, basil, parsley, dill, rosemary, olive oil, and capers. Sometimes, you will find zucchini with blossoms still attached. They are delightful stuffed and baked, and they make lovely sweet or savory fritters. Squash blossoms are delicate and should be prepared on the same day as purchase. Keep them in the refrigerator crisper until ready to use.

Index

Bold type indicates that a recipe has an accompanying photograph.

ACKNOWLEDGMENTS

Special thanks to my wife and editor in residence, Susan; our indispensable assistant and comrade, Mary Gilbert; and our friends and agents, Gene Winick and Sam Pinkus. Much appreciation also goes to Simon & Schuster, Scribner, and Weldon Owen for their devotion to this project. Thank you Carolyn, Susan, Bill, Marah, John, Terry, Roger, Gaye, Val, Norman, and all the other capable and talented folks who gave a part of themselves to the Joy of Cooking All About series.

My eternal appreciation goes to the food experts, writers, and editors whose contributions and collaborations are at the heart of Joy—especially Stephen Schmidt. He was to the 1997 edition what Chef Pierre Adrian was to Mom's final editions of Joy. Thank you one and all.

Ethan Becker

FOOD EXPERTS, WRITERS, AND EDITORS

Selma Abrams, Jody Adams, Samia Ahad, Bruce Aidells, Katherine Alford, Deirdre Allen, Pam Anderson, Elizabeth Andoh, Phillip Andres, Alice Arndt, John Ash, Nancy Baggett, Rick and Deann Bayless, Lee E. Benning, Rose Levy Beranbaum, Brigit Legere Binns, Jack Bishop, Carole Bloom, Arthur Boehm, Ed Brown, JeanMarie Brownson, Larry Catanzaro, Val Cipollone, Polly Clingerman, Elaine Corn, Bruce Cost, Amy Cotler, Brian Crawley, Gail Damerow, Linda Dann, Deirdre Davis, Jane Spencer Davis, Erica De Mane, Susan Derecskey, Abigail Johnson Dodge, Jim Dodge, Aurora Esther, Michele Fagerroos, Eva Forson, Margaret Fox, Betty Fussell, Mary Gilbert, Darra Goldstein, Elaine Gonzalez, Dorie Greenspan, Maria Guarnaschelli, Helen Gustafson, Pat Haley, Gordon Hamersley, Melissa Hamilton, Jessica Harris, Hallie Harron, Nao Hauser, William Hay, Larry Hayden, Kate Hays, Marcella Hazan, Tim Healea, Janie Hibler, Lee Hofstetter, Paula Hogan, Rosemary Howe, Mike Hughes, Jennifer Humphries, Dana Jacobi, Stephen Johnson, Lynne Rossetto Kasper, Denis Kelly, Fran Kennedy, Johanne Killeen and George Germon, Shirley King, Maya Klein, Diane M. Kochilas, Phyllis Kohn, Aglaia Kremezi, Mildred Kroll, Loni Kuhn, Corby Kummer, Virginia Lawrence, Jill Leigh, Karen Levin, Lori Longbotham, Susan Hermann Loomis, Emily Luchetti, Stephanie Lyness, Karen MacNeil, Deborah Madison, Linda Marino, Kathleen McAndrews, Alice Medrich, Anne Mendelson, Lisa Montenegro, Cindy Mushet, Marion Nestle, Toby Oksman, Joyce O'Neill, Suzen O'Rourke, Russ Parsons, Holly Pearson, James Peterson, Marina Petrakos, Mary Placek, Maricel Presilla, Marion K. Pruitt, Adam Rapoport, Mardee Haidin Regan, Peter Reinhart, Sarah Anne Reynolds, Madge Rosenberg, Nicole Routhier, Jon Rowley, Nancy Ross Ryan, Chris Schlesinger, Stephen Schmidt, Lisa Schumacher, Marie Simmons, Nina Simonds, A. Cort Sinnes, Sue Spitler, Marah Stets, Molly Stevens, Christopher Stoye, Susan Stuck, Sylvia Thompson, Jean and Pierre Troisgros, Jill Van Cleave, Patricia Wells, Laurie Wenk, Caroline Wheaton, Jasper White, Jonathan White, Marilyn Wilkenson, Carla Williams, Virginia Willis, John Willoughby, Deborah Winson, Lisa Yockelson.

Weldon Owen wishes to thank the following people for their generous assistance and support in producing this book: Desne Border, Ken DellaPenta, and Joan Olson.